THINK OPPOSITE

Advance Praise

"Simple. Truthful. Honest. Alison's story and business philosophy are on point to change and revolutionize the way of thinking for the entrepreneur from standard to exceptional."

—Dr. Alfredo Petrone

"I love the way Alison gently pulls you to think about things and situations differently. She utilizes her own personal experiences and then presents questions to assist with looking at situations differently. Alison also offers up scenarios for thinking differently in situations! Nice work."

—Kim Boudreau Smith, CEO, Bold Radio

"From the moment I learned about Domino Thinking, I was intrigued by it. Alison truly has a way of approaching our beliefs and actions that is well outside of conventional. Reading this book, I realized that this new way of approaching my world really could change my life, and help change the world. When it comes to making a difference with my business, I often feel discouraged. I am only one person. After reading this book, I cannot help but think that anything is possible."

—Lisa Smith

"Alison Donaghey asks us to think critically and intelligently. She invites us to think more freely and deliberately in ways that hold promise for better lives, better businesses, and a better world. This book will motivate you to consider thinking and acting to achieve results that matter."

—Susan Hess Nelson, PhD, Honorary Research Associate, Sociology Department & Global Studies Program, Vancouver Island University.

THINK OPPOSITE

Using The Domino Effect
to Change Your Business,
Change the World

ALISON DONAGHEY

NEW YORK

NASHVILLE • MELBOURNE • VANCOUVER

THINK OPPOSITE
Using The Domino Effect to Change Your Business, Change the World

Published in New York, New York, by Morgan James Publishing in partnership with Difference Press. Morgan James and The Entrepreneurial Publisher are trademarks of Morgan James, LLC. www.MorganJamesPublishing.com

The Morgan James Speakers Group can bring authors to your live event. For more information or to book an event visit The Morgan James Speakers Group at www.TheMorganJamesSpeakersGroup.com.

ISBN 978-1-68350-346-0 paperback
ISBN 978-1-68350-347-7 eBook
ISBN 978-1-68350-348-4 hardcover
Library of Congress Control Number:
2016918730

Shelfie

A **free** eBook edition is available with the purchase of this print book.

CLEARLY PRINT YOUR NAME ABOVE IN UPPER CASE

Instructions to claim your free eBook edition:
1. Download the Shelfie app for Android or iOS
2. Write your name in **UPPER CASE** above
3. Use the Shelfie app to submit a photo
4. Download your eBook to any device

Cover Design by:
Rachel Lopez
www.r2cdesign.com

Interior Design by:
Bonnie Bushman
The Whole Caboodle Graphic Design

Editing:
Grace Kerina

Author's photo courtesy of
Alicia Dewar Photography

In an effort to support local communities, raise awareness and funds, Morgan James Publishing donates a percentage of all book sales for the life of each book to Habitat for Humanity Peninsula and Greater Williamsburg.

Get involved today! Visit
www.MorganJamesBuilds.com

DEDICATION

Tone, you are my reason.

My parents, for being proud of me.

Tanya, for doing the stuff I don't want to do.

TABLE OF CONTENTS

Introduction

THERE'S NO GOING BACK NOW

"My goal in life is to make the biggest impact with the least amount of force."

—**Tone Donaghey**, my amazing son

Think Opposite

T*hink Opposite* is a concept I use all the time and some of you may already be using it and not even know it.

To *Think Opposite* means to *suspend* your belief just long enough to consider the opposite perspective. Just long enough to see that there is another side to that coin you call your point of view. In doing so we can make space for other people, their history, their point of view and it is in that space we are able to hold conversation, and who knows … we may learn something.

In using *Think Opposite* I have been able to have better conversations with people, build better connection, be less invested in the outcome of other people's choices or beliefs and more invested in the discussion and why we believe what we believe. When I *Think Opposite* I build personal credibility and therefore trust.

We have become so embedded in our tribes, which are echochambers for our point of view, that we obtain an inflated sense of "right-ness" about said beliefs because no one in our tribe disagrees with us. No one offers an opportunity for discussion which results in us losing our ability to converse with someone who we can learn from, who can learn from us.

For a healthy society we need to be able to talk about things and the first step is to *Think Opposite* because it allows us to see the point of view of the other. When we do that we can find a bit of understanding and from there we can communicate and build trust

Consider this: A man says to you "I don't care what anyone says, apples are the best fruit ever; better than all other fruits." At face value you may accept his statement but what if he then tells you he has never tried any other fruit. Do you still feel the same way about opinion? Do you trust him? If he has never considered another option he loses credibility and he has shut down any opportunity for discussion or growth.

Don't be the guy with the apple. Be the guy who has tried all the fruit and then make a decision based on all the information you gathered because you took the time to suspend your belief to consider an opposite perspective.

The Problem

If you are anything like me, life is busy and sometimes it feels like you are on a hamster wheel, going really fast to get nowhere.

There are so many demands on our time—the job, our own expectations, the expectations of others, boyfriends, wives, children, media, Facebook, bosses, employees. Whew! I am tired just listing all of that, let alone contemplating the effort that goes into doing it all.

How are we supposed to contribute to the overall good of our lives and the world if we can barely keep our heads above water? The world keeps spinning though and we have to figure out a way to understand it so that we can impact it in a favourable way.

These demands on our time and attention start happening at an early age and the skills are not being taught to cope with them. Realistically, how can teachers and parents teach kids how to handle this when a) they are not aware that it is happening and b) they don't have the skills to handle it in their own lives?

Our kids are not being taught in school to think critically and we don't have time or the skills to teach them, because we are too busy reacting to problems rather than thinking critically about them and finding solutions.

Our schools are set up to function best with the old way of life: The get-a-government-job, get-a-pension-and-health-plan, be-loyal-to-a-company-and-they-will-be-loyal-to-you way of putting in our time. This is a way that is rapidly disappearing. More and more companies are switching their employees to part-time to avoid having to pay benefits. Job security is a thing of the past and technology is replacing the need for humans in the workplace.

The problem is that we don't know how to live in this new world. We have been indoctrinated in the way things were and how we should behave in that system, but that system is disappearing and now we have to learn to play by a whole new set of rules. There is no rule book because one hasn't been written yet. (Hint: This means there's a great opportunity for you.)

Our world is changing so fast our lives are a blur. If we had the time to reflect, if we dared to take a pause and look around us, we might wonder where the life we were promised was. We might, if we took the time to think, wonder if the path we were on would lead us back to that early ideal, or if it was just leading us deeper into the wilderness.

What's the Cost?

We are becoming redundant and we don't even know it. Being *reactive* rather than *proactive* has become so normal we have convinced ourselves we are doing just fine, though we are not. There is a kind of insanity to being young and pursuing a job—like bank teller (I used to be a bank teller)—knowing most aspects of the job are becoming increasingly automated. Yet people keep applying for those jobs.

We are getting further and further into debt. We are chasing the next workshop that we think is going to give us freedom. We are armchair critics in world affairs, tossing simple solutions at complex problems and not understanding why there is a problem in the first place.

We are miserable. Somewhere inside us, we know we are settling for less. We are not living up to our own potential and we are teaching our children to settle too.

We are working for businesses, managing teams, or running our own businesses, but if we are not engaged, if we are living in limbo, somewhere between the old world and the new world. We are jeopardizing our relationships with our clients and alienating our staff, forcing them to become the very thing we are trying not to perpetuate. We are watching our communities suffer and the world bleed.

This costs us financially and worse, it costs us our integrity.

The New World

It's great that this is happening. Really. Now we are forced to be creative, to step outside of the norm and build lives we feel are worth living.

Building a life where we can make an impact in a world where we can be a part of the solution. Isn't that exciting?

You are already part of that. Through the simple act of reading this book you are indicating that you are searching for more. By searching, you are already breaking the chains that have bound you to the old world.

You will be happy to go to work in this new world. You will set an example for those around you and show them that they, too, can be part of it. You will be inspiring and you will connect to people who are engaged and happy to be doing business with you, to be beside you, and to be a part of your life.

Build your own new world, one that's based on your values and what brings you joy, and they will come.

To You

Thank you for thinking enough of yourself and the world around you to take this step toward critical, accountable thinking. It may not be easy, but I am doing it with you and so are many others.

It is through consciously working toward thinking critically and being solution-based that the world is going to thrive. We are not going to see results overnight, but then again, even the best of the best start somewhere and keep paying attention to the results they're getting as they go. Muhammad Ali, for example, didn't win his first fight,but through consistent improvement and awareness he became the best fighter of all time. He changed the world just by being the best version of himself.

Wise Words from My Peeps

At the beginning of each chapter I offer a quote by someone who's important to me, someone who has had an impact on my journey. I could have selected quotes from famous people, but I wanted to honour the people who have been part of my life, and show the brilliance in everyday people. People like them. People like you.

I promise that you are already making an impact, even without knowing it. You don't have to be Mother Theresa to make change happen. You just have to follow your own truth.

What You Can Expect

I'm going to start by telling you a little about myself. I'll tell you how my journey took me from the old world to the new and what it was like to throw away a lifetime of learned truth that wasn't…at least, not any more. The rest of the book is about how you can implement changes to create and step into your own new world. At the end, I'll alert you to some obstacles you may encounter and we'll take a look ahead.

At the end of every chapter is a section dedicated to promoting thought called "Domino Thinking When we start becoming aware of our thinking we become aware of the domino effect of those thoughts: one thought leads to the next **to the next** and they are all interdependent.

It's the interdependency, that mutual reliance, which is beautiful. This process is about the synergy of our thoughts and actions, which is a dance of sorts.

Each Domino Thinking section starts with a relatively simple idea or event and then asks you to really think about the implications. The purpose of these sections is to encourage you to practice thinking critically. Domino Thinking won't always relate to the chapter it concludes. It may, in fact, only be there to encourage a new direction of thought.

The benefits of the Domino Thinking sections are threefold:

First, when we focus on something, in this case the topic of the chapter, and then a random idea is thrown at us, like a Domino Thinking topic that's about something different, we are not expecting it, and our brains can surprise us with relevant connections between the chapter's topic and the topic of the Domino Thinking section. The purpose behind this is to trick our minds into thinking up useful ideas.

Second, once we have thought about the topics in the Domino Thinking section, we can apply this new way of thinking to our business in a more relatable way. It can be easier to accept a thought initially if it doesn't apply directly to what we are thinking or worrying about in our life. There is less ego involved and therefore we are more open to assimilating something new.

Third, selecting seemingly random situations to think about shows us how easy it is to start seeing the world from a different perspective—a critical thinking perspective. And because critical thinking is like candy for the brain, our brains will want more of it, and that leads to more new thoughts for creating a new world.

I would love to hear about your experiences with the Domino Thinking, and encourage you to share them with me on my website, Domino Thinking, at:

www.dominothinking.com/lets-talk

Congratulations for Wanting More

You are not an ordinary human. You are already ahead of the curve. The reality is that sometimes the path you are taking on will be hard, and people may not like the changes you make.

As you change and move toward your new world, you will start to attract new people who will make it easier for you to keep going. You will love the changes and will find your way with people who are also champions for change. You will be their leader.

Domino Thinking

This is your first of eleven Domino Thinking sections. Play around here. See what comes to mind as you read what's below. Write about it. Talk about it. Let thoughts about this pop into your head when you are driving or mulling over your morning coffee. Post your thoughts on Facebook and see what other people think. Revisit your thoughts about this Domino Thinking section after you're done this book and see if your thinking is the same.

Thinking will only take us so far. We cannot ultimately predict outcomes, but we can consider what we think and perhaps in doing so shape the outcome as we take action.

I was talking with a client about this book and about critical thinking in general and he said to me, "Remember that nursery rhyme that started, 'There was an old lady who swallowed a fly?'" I told him I did and we discussed how she went on to swallow all sorts of things, like spiders to catch the fly and cats to catch the spider and on and on.

He said he liked to think about it a bit differently. He calls his version "There was an old lady who swallowed a lie." We had a great conversation about the lies that we accept as truths and how we keep swallowing other lies to try to turn that first lie into something resembling the truth.

The reality is that a lie will never become a truth, but we muddy the original lie and pack so many things on top of it that we no longer remember what that original lie was or where it came from. But it has become part of who we are, just like the fly the old lady swallowed. The spider and the cat and the other items became part of who she was… right up until it killed her.

What lies have you swallowed? And what other lies have you told yourself to make those lies seem more believable? Who have you brought in on your lies? Have any of these statements been lies that have shown up in your life?

- Business has a certain way it needs to be run and you had better not deviate.
- Girls can't throw.
- Boys don't cry.
- You should want to get married.
- You should want to have kids.
- You have to work really hard to be successful.
- Postpone the good things in life until you retire.
- It's better to save than to spend.
- Work is not fun. If it were fun it wouldn't be called work.

Even if these don't apply to you, even if none of them have been lies in your life, pick one that caught your attention. Look at it. Think about what other lies a person who *did* swallow that lie may be telling themselves. If a person grew up being told that white was right and black was bad, what other lies would they have to tell themselves to believe it to be true? What media would they be more likely to believe? Who would they be friends with? Where would they live? Where would they travel? How far would they go to make that lie true?

Now look at your life and go backward with one of your beliefs that doesn't sit quite right with you. Maybe you don't get up and dance at parties because you think you would look stupid. What was the lie you had to swallow to make you have this thought? How many lies did you have to swallow to keep that thought going? Who do you keep in your life that confirms this lie to you? What would happen if you got up and danced instead?

Think about this: How does what you think about this situation apply in some way to your business? Come up with two instances of how you might be accepting or perpetuating lies.

Chapter 1
THE EXAMPLE OF ME

"Set a course and go. Don't wait. Do you know what happens to those that wait? Nothing. Nothing at all. It's only in motion that our lives take shape."

— **Eric Gilmer**, my oldest friend
and the reason I survived university

The Origin of Sonshine Girls Painting

U p until the time I was 19 I had never held a baby or been in the same room as one. I didn't understand them and, therefore, didn't really want one. It made sense that I was on the pill. So, you can imagine my surprise when I found out I was pregnant.

Whoever handed out babies must have messed that one up. Did they not know I wasn't built to be a mother? I swear, those who handed out babies realized the error of their ways and decided they had to make sure they gave me a really good child who would forgive me for my screw-ups.

I struggled as a single parent for a few years. I took a lot of dead-end jobs, making minimum wage, and finally decided to go to university so I could get a "good" job. That was possibly a lie I bought into. I am still debating that.

I enrolled full-time and got a diploma in criminology. Then I started a Bachelor of Arts degree with a double minor in psychology and sociology. I was working three jobs to make ends meet when I met a guy who was a house painter. We started dating and he told me he could teach me how to paint and I could make more money and work less so I could see my son more. That seemed like a great idea to me.

He and I were together for six years, which was six years longer than it should have been. He died in 1999 of a brain disease. I had to go on welfare and I was in huge debt from his drug addiction. I had no idea what to do and I dropped out of university in my third year due to a bad illness. I was lost.

I decided to start my own painting company. How hard could it be? I named my company Sonshine Girls Painting, because of my son and because, when he was little, I sang songs about sunshine like "You Are My Sunshine," and "I've got Sunshine". I included "Girls" in the name because I was tired of being told that girls couldn't do things. This way, people would know in advance that I was female and if they didn't think girls could do things, then they were free to go elsewhere.

Starting the painting business was hard, but I was good at it, and within a couple of months I was off of welfare. Within a year, I had staff working for me and was able to go back to school to finish my BA. Business kept getting better. But there was always this voice inside me urging me to do something more, to make more of a difference in the world.

The Origin of Domino Thinking

Over the years, I have been asked to speak at programs for youth in the trades and at high schools for career planning events. As those invitations became more frequent I thought I should join Toastmasters and get some more practice with public speaking.

Although I loved what I learned at Toastmasters, I didn't get really excited about the Toastmasters type of speaking. Then I gave a speech on feminism, and then one on voting, and yet another on racism. I realized I enjoyed talking about controversial topics. I loved asking people to think about things and to notice the domino effect of their thinking. *That* was my *thing*.

I spoke at a women's conference about how we are not as far along in the evolution of equality as we think we are. Afterwards, people came up to me and said, "I never thought of it that way," and "Boy, I have some thinking to do." I knew I had made a difference to many of the women in that room.

I realized it would be nice to do more things like that, but I had a painting business to run and a mortgage to pay and staff to think about. Who was I to talk to people about thinking, anyway?

About a week after the women's conference, a woman I know called me and asked what I was going to do about being such a great speaker and having a unique view of the world. I gave her some feeble responses, but she insisted that I do something. A couple of days later, she told me she'd had a great idea for a radio show that would get me more involved in the speaking world. Pretty soon I had a name for a new business—Domino Thinking—and a semblance of a plan.

At a women's conference in New York, I heard Angela Lauria speak about her company, The Author Incubator, and I realized that if I was going to be serious about Domino Thinking and asking people to think more critically about their businesses and their lives, I needed to write a book. Here it is.

My Nay-Says

Despite how easily my story can be told, it was not an easy journey to live. I was told I couldn't be a single parent. I was told I couldn't be a woman in the trades. I was told I should be grateful for the life I had and not want too much more. I was told I shouldn't talk about topics that might make people uncomfortable. Those voices lived in my head all the time.

Looking back, I see a pattern in my life. For a while, I would listen to the voices of other people saying I couldn't do more and so I stuck with minimum-wage jobs. Then I noticed another voice in my head that told me I could do better.Soon that little voice yelled at me louder than the other voices, until I made the decision to go back to school and strive for more. Then I heard the voices of others telling me I should settle for that, stop there. Again, before long, that little voice saying I could do better was screaming louder and so I started Sonshine Girls Painting. The voices were under control a bit for a while then. I was feeling successful. I was okay with the nay-sayers. Every once in a while I would hear that tiny voice tell me I was settling and that I could do more. Guess what? Yep! Eventually it got louder and that's when I started Domino Thinking.

What helped me a lot was having people around who believed in me when I didn't believe in myself. They stretched my comfort zone and gave me a place to be scared and still move forward.

I remember one time when I was pumping gas into my old beat-up painting van at the end of a workday. I was in my painting clothes, my hair was pulled up in a bandana, and I was tired. There was a beautiful woman in a sports car in front of me at the pumps. She was well dressed. Her make-up was perfect. Her hair was long and silky. By comparison I felt rather inadequate.

And then that little, quiet voice in my head said to me, "But Sonshine Girls *hires* people. We give people *jobs* so they can pay their rent and do some of the things they *love* to do. We have great customers who *love* us. We give great *value* to our customers." I listened to that voice and I smiled at the lady. She gave me a smile back. To my surprise, she pointed at the logo on my van and gave me a thumbs up.

I learned then that:

1. I never knew where encouragement might come from. It would show up in the most unusual places and at the oddest times, and I should be open to receiving it. I learned to be kinder to myself.
2. Sometimes, when I would expect encouragement, none showed up, and I learned the dangers of expectation.
3. Sometimes what was once an inspiration ceased being an inspiration. I learned to adapt.

In the early days, my son helped me push forward. Every time I felt like giving up I would look at him and think about what he saw when he looked at me and I would say to myself, "Is that who I want him to be—someone who gives up?" Eventually, I didn't need to do that anymore. He got older, but then I needed to find another reason for pushing forward.

Sonshine Girls Painting was doing really well. It seemed though, that I had settled into a life that on a scale of one to ten, was a seven. I felt that I was successful and I was showing my son success. The truth was, I was settling. It was probably good for me to settle at that point in time for a while; I had been fighting for such a long time. I needed a rest. But then the little voice in my head said, "Hey, what are you going to do for *you* now? What are you going to do for this *world*? This gig is good, but is it lighting up your soul? Is a seven out of ten good enough? I want a ten out of ten life."

Honestly, I had no idea *what* lit me up. Some days many things did; other days nothing at all did. I often felt lost. I knew

I had something else inside of me. I didn't know what it was, but I knew it didn't look like what I already had or anything I could see around me.

I Did It My Way

I love Frank Sinatra and when I was finding life hard I would play his song "My Way." I still do. I take the roof off my Jeep, blast Frank on my stereo, and sing my little heart out while driving to my next appointment.

It feels good to be in Frank's company. He reminds me that I do things the way I want to. I run my company in an atypical way and when it is time to pursue something else I am doing it my way too.

I sometimes forget that my way was a good way. When I do lose sight of that, I go back to my Jeep and spend some time with Frank. I get inspired again and regain my confidence.

The hard thing about doing it my way was that there were not a lot of people to emulate. So I got in the habit of watching out for things people were doing that I admired and then tweaking them to work for me. My friend Line would send me speaker's videos to listen to, or information about companies that were doing amazing work, or articles that were relevant to things I was speaking about.I would feel like I had a circle of influence through those people she pointed out to me.

I would watch how other companies did things and try to improve on it. I would pay attention to how I was treated by other companies or how I felt after doing business with them and I would do better. I took every opportunity to learn from everything around me.

Why I Am Doing This?

Ever since I was little I've seen things differently than my friends did. I got in trouble in class because I continued to ask, "Why?" long after all my friends stopped asking. I always wanted an explanation. As we know, our schools were not built for that.

I went through high school in trouble all the time for challenging my teachers. I had a hard time making friends because my friends didn't want to *think* about things. They just wanted to be teenagers. In retrospect, I did have friends, but at the time I mostly felt ostracized.

I organized a rally in high school to protest the teachers striking, because I didn't think it was fair that the guys who had been practising rugby all season weren't allowed to play because the teachers were on a work-to-rule strike, which meant no coaching. Those boys had worked so hard, as had other students in other departments.

At university I argued with teachers that my grade should not be attached to my attendance. I got good grades and handed work in on time. *That* should have determined my grades. Not how many times my ass was in a chair.

I argued with the cops who pulled me over because I had no doors on my Jeep. So what? The Jeep was still safer in an accident than a motorcycle. Their response was, "Well, the Jeep came with doors.", as if that was a reason. It had also come with a roof and I didn't have that on, so why wouldn't that same rule apply to the doors as well?

It has always been a part of me to want to make sense of things, to really think about things, and to want other people to think about things too. I've always seen how it makes life better whenever I take the time to think, to not accept something at face value and to question the status quo. When I look at the world and the problems in it, from big-world problems to personal challenges, almost all of it could be made better by thinking. I don't mean quick-fix thinking; I mean the critical stuff: *Where am I coming from? Where am I headed? Is that where I really want to go? Is my thinking today sound enough to get me there?*

I feel as though I've had no other choice but to make Domino Thinking my business. I needed to write this book and put the concept and practice of critical thinking at the core of my business and the speeches I give.

Client Success Stories

When I work with individuals or groups, they come away saying they hadn't thought of the topic the way I explained it. They *want* to look at things differently, maybe not the same way I look at things, which is totally fine, but in a way that feels more true or complete to them. They want to look for win-win situations. They want to make sure that what they are doing is fair to all concerned, and they want to be moving in a forward direction, making their world and *the* world a better place.

After you finish this book, I want you to experience those outcomes too. Read this book, see where your present thinking may be failing you, and say to yourself, "Hmmm, I never thought about it that way," and then go make beautiful changes.

Domino Thinking

Here is another opportunity for you to think about something in a different way. Think about how the aspects of the situation below may apply to your life, and how you may be able to look at things through the eyes of another person.

A woman I know went to Haiti with her ten-year-old daughter. They met quite a few very poor girls her daughter's age. When they realized that those girls had never been inside a hotel or played by a swimming pool, they brought them into the hotel so they could spend the day by the pool.

My friend told me this like she thought I would be impressed. I wasn't. All I could think about was that those girls may have had the best day of their life at ten years old, but have no means to recreate it.

Perhaps some of those girls would adapt and be happy going without having that experience again, but what if some of those girls made poor choices in order to get back into that hotel?

I asked myself, *what could have been better?*

I wondered if we have the right to introduce things to people without considering the long-term effects.

What might have happened if my friend had, instead, asked those girls to teach her how to make Haitian food? She could have bought the food from local people—giving them income for their families. She would have empowered those girls by showing them they had value and confirming that they already had skills. She could have met others in the community and fed them too, and what a different experience for her and her daughter that might have been.

Can you think of other things she could have done if she had thought of the possible long-term effects of her actions?

Think about this: How does what you think about this situation apply in some way to your business? Come up with two example of when you've acted without thinking about the outcome?

Chapter 2
THE SWEET SOLUTION

"Once we remove the costume of victimhood that we have so eagerly adorned most of our lives, for a while we may feel raw, vulnerable, and exposed. Rest assured, you will emerge into beautiful colours that are pure and aligned with your soul purpose and journey."

— **Jivi Saran**, my mindful guru who keeps it real

T he solution is simple.

Think.

I am not saying it is easy, but it is simple. Most of the mistakes we make are from lack of thinking. When we don't think we don't collect the information we need to make informed decisions. The reason we don't collect the information is two-fold.

First, we don't know we need information, because we didn't think further than the first solution we came up with. If we don't *think* more deeply, more critically, about the problem, we don't realize that there is more information needed.

Here's an example. Let's pretend a person—we will call him Bill—has developed an increase in thirst and urination. Bill thinks it's because of the weather and keeps drinking more water. If he's drinking more water it makes sense that he has to pee more. Right?

Maybe.

Or maybe not.

Maybe Bill has diabetes.

If he was willing to think more about the changes he's experiencing, he could find some answers that would help him more.

Second, the reason we tend to not think beyond the first solution is that we are busy. We live busy lives with lots of things going on that demand our attention. Even when we know we need more information, we think we are too busy to gather it.

Bill vaguely remembered reading something about increased thirst and urination being a sign of diabetes.He noticed that he'd been losing weight and was more tired than usual, but he just doesn't have the time to stop and look into it further. Perhaps if he didn't need to pee so often he would have more time, right?

Maybe.

Or maybe not. We often *react* to situations rather than actually *thinking* about them. How many illnesses could be avoided if we were proactive rather than reactive?

How does this lack of thinking show up in other areas of our lives? Our child starts to get withdrawn and we chalk it up to *him being a teenager*. Or our partner is staying at the office longer and we tell ourselves that *she's just catching up on work*. Or our best friend has lost 30 pounds and we don't notice until he points it out.

What is happening that makes us stop being present in our own lives? In order to start thinking critically we have to start being present.

If you break a situation down and take the time to *think about it*, you will discover that taking the time to think *saves* time, relationships, money, and your health in the long run.

I'll give you a business example of not taking the time to *think*, how it costs money and inevitably has a negative effect on stress levels.

Susan has a great sales rep for her retail store and they have worked together for a while. He introduces Susan to a new product and says it's going to be hot and she need to get in on the ground floor before her competition picks up on it.

Susan knows that her rival down the road has beat her to the punch quite a bit lately. She's not very happy about that and is desperate to put a stop to it. She's busy, so she makes a quick decision to add that new product line to her store. She's not as sure about the product as she'd like to be, but she trusts her rep. She already knows the perfect place to put the new product. She signs the contract and gets back to work.

A week later, a truck shows up with four huge boxes of this product. *Whoa*, she only wanted a couple units to test the waters with, but now she has a hundred. She has nowhere to put all the stock and she can't send it back. That bit was in the contract, which she didn't read: the minimum order was four boxes.

Susan argues with the delivery guy for a while and finally has to accept it. She calls her rep and he has no idea what's going on but will get back to her.

She is freaked out because she can't afford to pay for this entire order. Her staff is trying to look on the bright side, but she is too stressed to see that. She goes into her office while her staff tries to figure out what to do with the boxes.

In the meantime, in the furor, they all missed connecting with a client who walked in and tried to get some help, but then left angry at the lack of service.

This mistake takes weeks of time-sucking phone calls and transfers to try to deal with, and at the end Susan is stuck with the product. It's not nearly as hot as she'd hoped. Her rep is apologetic and sincerely hates that he led her astray. Her staff is annoyed at her attitude and their productivity has declined.

Do you see how taking the time to *think* (more about this in Chapter 3) rather than react would have been so much simpler and less stressful for Susan? How much money and time was lost because of her hasty decision? How badly morale was damaged?

One of the best ways to avoid these sorts of setbacks is to know what your big *Hell Yeah!* is (Chapter 4). You know:

that feeling you get when you have done an amazing job that *Wow-I–was-in-my-zone-and-I-felt-like-I-was-doing-something-with-impact* feeling. That is your *Hell Yeah!* I want you to feel that way more often than not.

Once you identify your *Hell Yeah!* you will know better how to effectively understand your customers, identify your impact points, and optimize your points of contact. This is important because if you are not connected to your *Hell Yeah!* you are not connected to your customer, so how will your customer be connected to you?

It helps to figuratively *Get In Bed With Your Customer* (Chapter 5) to really understand their needs and wants. It helps to start a love affair with your customers because, unless you have one of those very rare businesses whose customers need you more than you need them, you need to love your customers. Get inside their heads like you would a lover's. Once you have this sorted, you can set out a strategy that is in line with your *Hell Yeah!*

Additionally, until you know your *Hell Yeah!*, how will your *staff* be connected to you? How will they know the best way to show up at work or even if they like their job? We often hire people to do a job and then don't let them do it the way they are built to do it. Get to know your staff and then *Let Your Staff Be Kick-Ass* (Chapter 6). Get them on board with your vision, the way you want to relate to your customers, and then set them free to be creative and bold. You will be surprised how well they will do. If they don't do well, then you are better off without them—and they are better off without you.

You are going to be so damn proud of your *Hell Yeah!* that you'll want everyone to know it. Align yourself with community activities or groups that align with your vision and get behind them so that you *Love Where You Live* (Chapter 7).

Finally, this new way of thinking is going to impact the world because your business is a tool to make that happen, and *The World Needs You* (Chapter 8). You can take your vision globally in everything you do and with everything you expect—from your interactions with others to the businesses you support. You can take your *Hell Yeah!* on the road and travel to learn other ways of doing things and expand your brain.

You are going to encounter problems and obstacles (that's life) as you use thinking to improve your business and make a new world, but we will get you to *Dump The Nay-Say* (Chapter 9) and think in advance about what those obstacles might be and how you are going to resolve them.

You can see business as a tripod, with customers, staff, and community as each of the legs. On the top of the tripod is a camera through which you can see the world in clear focus. Along the way, as you think and create, you are going to have to deal with lighting issues and moving objects from here to there to get a better picture of things, but you will have new thought patterns to help you deal with the issues that come up. As you learn and put more thinking into your business, you will *Fly, Baby, Fly* (Chapter 10).

So keep turning these pages and together we will think about what you think about! We are heading out on a great adventure and I am super excited to be on this journey with you.

Domino Thinking

I met a woman who doesn't like to give money to the homeless because she doesn't know what they are going to do with it. Instead, she keeps granola bars in her car and when she sees a homeless person on the side of the road, like by a stoplight, with a sign on a piece of old cardboard that says, "I need money, please," she calls them over and gives them a granola bar. She told me that there was a homeless guy who wasn't grateful for the granola bar and she couldn't understand why.

Why wasn't he grateful? What assumptions did the woman make? Were there dangers in her thinking? Could the situation have been handled differently?

Would you see the situation differently if the sign had said, "Food please?" or, "Looking for work" or, "Money for beer"?

Take some time to really think about this and maybe at your next dinner party bring it up. Get other people to think about it too. What does your husband or wife think? How about your children?

Sometimes this Domino Thinking is best done through discussions, because verbalizing things out loud creates more clarity, and talking it over with others provides exposure to ideas that may be fresh to you, and it gets other people around you thinking more.

Think about this: How does what you think about this situation apply in some way to your business? Come up with two ideas about how you make assumptions.

Chapter 3
THINK

"We admire, even idolize, those who think critically and originally. But somehow those damn committees keep creeping up, using big words and protocol to disguise their homogeneous, milquetoast thoughts, and squash the spirit of the independents."

— **Marc Stoiber**, brilliant speech developer

I n order for humanity to thrive we require critical thinking. It is not a luxury for those who have time. It is a necessity. It is our responsibility to stop making excuses and to make time to think.

I get it. I really do. Life is busy. But if you start thinking critically you will come to embrace it as common practice. It will become easier and your results will be rewarding. You will become known for your ability to think, analyse, and come up with viable solutions. You will thrive and by default, so will the people around you.

Why Critical Thinking Is Needed

We used to be much better at thinking critically when our immediate survival depended on it. Back in the day, when we were realizing we needed each other to survive, people created tribes, groups of people who relied on each other's ideas. We didn't just survive, either, but expanded; in population, geography, and intelligence. If they were unable to consider all the opinions and needs of their members, there was a pretty good chance they would not survive. They needed their peacemakers and warriors, their smart and not-so-smart (sometimes not-so-smart people come up with the most brilliant ideas) tribe members. They needed their males and females, their shy folk and outgoing folk, and everything in between in order to create a healthy community.

When they were faced with famine, the whole community was a resource for coming up with solutions, which would be based on the individual's strengths and perspectives. When they faced saber-toothed tigers, there was brain *and* brawn behind their solution. If it didn't, it was snack time for the tiger. Living in a tribe meant doing things holistically. Everyone was needed.

That is not to say everyone always got along and it was always rainbows and butterflies. Life was tough and people got on each other's nerves, but they understood the importance of collaborating and communicating with others who didn't share their opinion.

Imagine this. If a tribe was from the north and someone in charge suggested it was a good idea to walk south and never stop and never question it, what would that look like? They would lose people to the cold harsh climate of the mountains, run out of food, and perhaps lose others to dangerous rival tribes. They would finally find themselves in the south close to the equator, where they would be in heat so foreign to them that they would lose many more members to heat stroke. They would eventually hit ocean and keep walking until the remaining few drowned.

Yes, it's an extreme example, but you can see how badly they needed someone at the very beginning to say, "No, that's ludicrous. We don't know how to survive in the mountains." If they were ignored at the beginning, they might say at each step of the way, "No, this is still ludicrous. We've already lost twenty percent of the tribe and for what?" and keep bringing the subject up until enough people stopped to listen. Those *questioners* would be the ones to save the tribe from blindly following an insane leader.

Are you prepared to be the person who stands up and says "No, this is ludicrous," or are you going to be the person who marches into the water because that was the way you were told it should be done?

What Critical Thinking Is Not

Critical thinking is not a one-sided, passed-down-through-the-generations habit. It is not the adoption of a homogenous point of view, and it is not acting on impulse or out of habit.

More and more we are putting ourselves into these online "tribes". We think we are moving ourselves forward, and maybe it is moving our particular point of view forward, but what if our point of view is wrong? I mean, *extreme* Muslims rally behind their point of view, as do KKK members and neo-Nazis. They are so certain they are right that they will kill to preserve their point of view. Does their fanatical devotion to their idea give it authority instead of make it right?

We have extremely polarised political parties that are so certain they are right that they don't consider the views from the opposition across the floor. They dismiss objections because of the source of the objection, not because the objection is invalid. If it's not a thought that belongs to their homogenous tribe it's not a thought worth listening to.

Where in your life are you excluding other ideas in order to protect your own? I heard a man once say, "Why not listen to someone else? What do I have to lose?" So, what do *you* have to lose?

The Benefits of Critical Thinking

Critical thinking is the opposite of group thinking. Critical thinking is eclectic and it challenges the status quo. Always.

The benefit of critical thinking is that it allows for ideas and innovation to develop. How did the Wright brothers come up with a working plane when others could not? They refused to accept the status quo of "we cannot fly"—and now we are flying people to Mars.

Rosa Parks refused to accept the status quo and would not relinquish her seat on the bus. Her action resulted in a movement toward racial equality.

What would life have been like without those people and their critical thoughts and resulting actions?

Critical thinking has propelled civilization forward from one innovation to the next, always accompanied by a struggle with the status quo of the time. It's what makes one company excel at customer service while its counterpart, a company that goes along accepting the status quo, drops the ball and loses customers.

The Problem with Homogenous Thinking

Homogenous, or non-critical thinking is easy. We like to belong to groups that become echo chambers for our ideas. Other people's ideas, when they differ from our own, often cause confrontation, and that can be scary. So we follow the leaders, and we put the leaders of our groups on pedestals and don't question them.

Didn't people do this with Hitler—see him as a hero who was going to create more jobs? And then they blindly followed him, turned in their Jewish friends, and pulled the levers in the gas chambers. What about how Pol Pot destroyed Cambodia without anyone intervening for four years? There were over two million deaths in Cambodia during that time—21% of the population. When we make a comment about "drinking the Kool-Aid," do we stop and think about Jim Jones and how more than 900 of his followers committed suicide?

Those things happened because of leaders who told their followers to walk in a certain direction and not stop for anything. People obeyed. Those leaders didn't start out as the monsters they became. It all started with one misguided decision and no one questioned them, or not enough people questioned them, until their ideas grew to epic proportions and much damage had been done.

In 1961, there was a famous study done by psychologist Stanley Milgram, which was aptly called the Milgram Experiment. Its intent was to study how authority impacted a person's ability to disobey. Disturbingly, Milgram found that a high level of people obeyed, even if they thought they were causing harm and, at times, death.

How do we allow this kind of following-without-thinking to happen? Why do we not disobey? It's because we are conditioned to follow the status quo and the status quo tells us not to question.

How do these situations I've just written about, that may seem to exist outside of your present reality, affect you? The more we become complacent in our thinking, the more we are at risk of allowing bad things to happen. It helps to have some examples as reminders.

We start making a difference by thinking about what we think about.

While the examples above are about global issues, they still apply to your life and your business. What things are you accepting as okay, even if they intuitively feel wrong?

- Policies at your children's schools? Are they serving your child? Other parents? The teachers?
- Your family dynamics? Is there a power struggle? Who is it serving?
- How to give to charity? What do they do with your contributions?

When you don't address those nagging little queries in your head, what is the fallout? What are you passively approving? What are you settling for, and what message are you sending to the world?

Silence is compliance.

What are you agreeing to by your silence?

The solution starts with remembering that you have a voice.

The Solution

We need to think critically. We need to surround ourselves with opportunities to prove or disprove our theories, so that we can look at things from all sides and make better decisions. It is curiosity and probing that allows us to keep what works and throw out what does not; it's how we say, "No, this is ludicrous."

Remember when you were little and you wanted to know things? Why does mom wear a skirt and dad doesn't? Why does Johnny have two moms? Why is the sky blue? Why does that man have brown skin—did he stay out in the sun too long without sunscreen? Why? Why? *Why?*

We are born knowing how to question.

Because of our parents (because who has time for all those 'whys'?) and our schools (teachers have a lot of students to teach and the curriculum is not geared towards individuality but conformity, we stop asking why.) We stop verbalizing our innate curiosity and we go along to get along. Then we find ourselves in jobs or owning our own businesses where we are expected to toe the line and follow the "best practices" without asking what makes them the best.

What would have happened if Eleanor Roosevelt hadn't used her status to bring awareness to injustices? The "best practice" for a woman of her social standing at that time was to be a good debutante, not to stand up for black rights or equality for women.

Woody Guthrie used his talent as a singer and songwriter to shine a light on migrant workers and unions. The "best practice" in his time was to make pop songs.

Harvey Milk was pivotal in promoting gay rights awareness in San Francisco. The "best practice" in his time was to stay in the closet.

Ralph Nader should have kept quiet about fighting for a better environment.

Following the "best practices" of their times, continuing to do the expected things rather than thinking critically and doing something new, different, better, would mean Muhammad Ali should have just stuck to fighting; Billie Jean King should have become a housewife, not a Wimbledon champion vying for gender equality; Michael Moore should have made Disney movies not drawn attention to corporate outsourcing, healthcare, or gun control.

Do you see why we needed these people? Do you see why we need *you*? Do you see how you are not alone?

I am sure it wasn't easy for those people or anyone else who rocked the boat, but the payoffs are *huge*.

The human race needs us to step outside the status quo. Think about what is happening and if it reallyis the best way. What are you doing to become known for the impact you are going to make on the world? You have something in you. I know you do. Yyou have the capacity to change lives, to make the world better.

So forget what you think you know and what the tribe is telling you. Remember who you were as a child and remember your early love affair with the word why.

Domino Thinking

There is a natural disaster in a third world country. A tsunami hit and the news is showing families who have lost their homes. They are being captured on camera wandering around the rubble looking for their missing family members or trying to salvage something of their homes. There are small children who are crying in the middle of a torn-up region that used to be a town, and the camera keeps showing close-ups of their faces and emphasizing how they are alone. There is a cry for volunteers from search and rescue and disaster relief organizations. A bunch of Western parents (most likely women) all over North America start to gather up stuffed animals to send to these poor children to help console them in their time of loss and need.

What do you think about what those women choose to collect and send?

Is it helping or hurting?

Is it an ego-driven solution—something that serves the giver but not the receiver?

Why do you think those women think what they're doing is a solution to a complex problem like a land ravaged by a tsunami?

Where do those stuffed animals actually go when they land in the third-world country?

What would those women tell their friends after collecting the stuffed animals?

What would be a different solution?

If you have a solution why would it be better?

How would the lives of these women in North America be different with your solution? How about the lives of those kids in the third-world country?

What would those women say about your solution?

We often act on good intentions—but you know what they say about good intentions: they pave the road to hell. I am asking you to no longer accept good intentions as **su**fficient reasoning for action, or to ignore the ramifications of an action. Are we going to get it right every time if we do that? No; but when we bring awareness and a questioning mindset into situations, we certainly improve our chances of getting things right for more people more often.

Think about this: How does what you think about this situation apply in some way to your business? Come up with two ideas of how you are not thinking things through.

Chapter 4
HELL YEAH!

"Purpose is the distinction between ordinary and extraordinary. It is the driving force that makes your goals non-negotiable. It makes you unstoppable and guarantees eventual success regardless of any circumstances."

— **Anel Bester**, my "give fear the finger" coach

Why are you doing what you are doing? Spoiler alert. That *why* is what floats your boat, curls your toes, flies your flag. Your answer will not be something you would hear in business school. For the time being, forget your five-year plan. Seriously. Those may work for some people and they have a place, but this is not that place. That is a whole other book.

FYI I have never had a five-year plan, which is good, because where I was in 1995 (welfare), 2000 (starting a business), 2005 (travelling to Africa and Europe), 2010 (designing a house) and 2015 (rocking my life by starting Domino Thinking) was nowhere where I'd have been able to predict I would be five years before. *Life happened.*

What did stay consistent in was my *vision*. I didn't know at the time that it was a vision, but in retrospect I can see that I had a *Hell Yeah!* and it was leading me.

Why Your *Hell Yeah!* Is Needed

You need to know your *Hell Yeah!* because that will steer all your choices. Who you market to, hire, learn from, support in your community, and how you show up in the world. Once you understand what is motivating you to do what you do, you can make decisions with ease. If you don't know, then you flounder all over the place, create a mess of work, and present a disorderly impression.

Whether you are self-employed, the CEO of a big company, or a barista at Starbucks, your *Hell Yeah!* is why you get up in the morning to go to work. Your choices align with your *Hell Yeah!* and your *Hell Yeah!* informs you on how to present yourself to your co-workers, your staff, and your customers. There is something magical that happens when we can identify why we are doing something, and it makes all our decisions easier.

You will find that when your *Hell Yeah!* is in alignment with who you are, you will always be striving to move in that direction, in your personal life and in your professional life.

If you don't know what pushes you forward, you cannot convey it to your customers, staff, and community. You will just be another business without a soul.

Think of your vision as your compass. Your vision will keep you on track. When you get stressed out or have to deal with life's tragedies; when you get tired or are overcome with excitement you can pull out your vision compass and remember where you are going.

Write down your *Hell Yeah!* Talk about it. Put it in the signature in your emails. Dedicate a page on your website to explaining the history of it. Get a tattoo. Whatever you have to do that works for you to connect with it, just do it. There is no right way to engage with your *Hell Yeah!* except that it must works for you.

For my house painting business, I bring up my *Hell Yeah!* when I give my estimates. With my Domino Thinking business, when I am asked what I do I always say, "I challenge people to think about what they think about," and that opens a door to conversation.

Find a place to plant your vision that will have the most impact and dig that hole, plant it, water it, and watch it grow. Don't just plant it and leave it. Talk to it. Ask it to help you with tough decisions. *Nurture* it.

What Your *Hell Yeah!* Is Not

Let's not confuse your *Hell Yeah!* (your vision) with your *reason* for doing what you do. They may be different.

My Sonshine Girls Painting *Hell Yeah!* is to have a company in the trades that excels at customer service, but my *reason* for the business was my son, my need for autonomy, a way to pay bills and buy food to put on the table. With Domino Thinking, my *Hell Yeah!* is to get people to think about what they think about, but my *reasons* for doing that business are that I want to travel, I want to speak, and I want to help people rock their businesses. I do all of that by getting people to *Think Opposite.*

Vision is not about fundamental needs. Your vision is your legacy. *Reason* has more to do with what you need in the moment. I need to book more jobs because I want to go on a trip, or I had to pay for a new paint sprayer, or I needed to hire a coach to improve my speaking. Those are reasons. However, my vision guides how I get those extra jobs. It's the moral compass of my company.

At the beginning, when times were tough, sometimes I was tempted to overbid a job because I really needed money. That was my reason—to price the job high so I could pay bills. My vision ensured that I didn't overcharge, because that would have been out of alignment with my legacy, my *Hell Yeah!* When I make those legacy choices I get a *Hell Yeah!* happening in my body. When I was conflicted and reverted back to *Hell Yeah!* and away from my *reason*, I felt good about staying focused on the bigger picture of building a reputable company, one that didn't overbid.

Ironically, often on jobs where I really struggled between my reasons and my vision, I'd get tips from my clients at the end of the job, or amazing referrals, and more money than I'd expected would come in, and the bills got paid.

What is your vision and what are your reasons? This is an important distinction. Where do they fall out of alignment? Once you understand the difference, you will understand your motives when faced with a decision.

Take the time to write out your *Hell Yeah!* and your reasons for being in business., so that you know the difference and can access it easily.

The Benefits of Having a *Hell Yeah!*

My vision for the painting company was that I wanted my clients to enjoy the journey and feel like they mattered to me, because they did. I wanted to base my business on a high percentage of referrals. Let's face it, painting houses is not rocket science, and there were a lot of painters in town. Reality check: The trades are not known for their customer service. My *Hell Yeah!* filled that gap.

Now that I know more about myself (that happens as we get older), I realize that my vision was and is about educating and learning. My desire to have my clients experience the best I could provide was about wanting to educate them. I would learn what they needed and give them as much information as I could, so that they could make an informed decision. I would give detailed estimates so that they knew how their money was being spent. I found that when people felt informed, they also felt cared for.

With Domino Thinking, yes, I challenge people to think about what they think about, but my underlying vision is still about educating and learning. I learn so much from people, and when I ask them to think they learn things about themselves.

They can choose to take time to become more informed. This is why I do mastermind groups, strategize, and speak. One day I will be involved in crafting a new school system. It's all in line with my vision.

How does my vision of educating and learning impact my personal life? I have friends who I learn from. I have conversations that make me want to be a better person. If I am still talking about the weather five minutes into a conversation, I tend to extract myself. I am busy, and know what I want. I want to be stimulated and I want to challenge others to do the same.

Your *Hell Yeah!* is what is going to make you unique in your field and help you grow your business.

The Problem with Not Having A *Hell Yeah!*

I did a coaching session with an elite athlete about him obtaining sponsorship and how he should go about it. I listened to him and couldn't figure out why a business would support him, so I asked him, "Why would someone give you money?" He responded with, "Well, I love golf." My response was, "So what?" We had some work to do on his vision.

We talked for a while and came up with something different for him to say. We found his vision. When he was young, his father died of obesity and he vowed he would never allow that to happen to himself. He became really active and tried all types of sports. He felt team sports weren't for him, as he preferred solo sports. When he found golf, he found a safe place to think and a way to stay healthy. His vision was to use exercise to combat obesity. Then he had something he could market—and someone he could market it to.

Help to Find Your *Hell Yeah!*

What do you do if you're not sure what your vision is? I suspect that you actually do know. We are always so much smarter than we think we are. I also suspect that you think it should be more complicated than it truly is.

Maybe your vision is to have a life of quiet solitude, so you go on yoga retreats, spend time in your backyard in your garden, and read a lot of books. Or maybe you want to change the medical system. Or be the highest-paid person under 40 in your firm. All valid goals—but my question is *why* do you want that?

I suggest you look at the times when you were happiest. What is the theme? I know I get jazzed when I am engaged in philosophical talks, and when I travel I love meeting local people and learning what they do and how they live. When do you get jazzed? Not those times you are *supposed* to be happy, like when you're with your kids or your wife or… or… or… Is it when you're mowing your lawn? Working on your car? Closing a big deal? In the middle of a party?

Then ask yourself *why* are you happiest there and then?

Let's take an example of a guy named Sam working on his car. Is he happy doing that because he is solving problems? Making something old new again? Is it because he used to do it with his dad and so he feels closer to his dad when he is working on the car? Is it because he feels a sense of accomplishment?

Let's look more closely at the example of Sam feeling closer to his dad. Why? Is it because Sam values family and connection? Because it gives him a sense of connection to his faith? Is it because he values the way his dad taught him how to do things?

Let's say it's because he values family and connection. How does that reveal itself in other ways? Oh, right! He spends lots of time with his staff cultivating relationships. He knows everything his staff does on their weekends and the sports their children play. And he always remembers his customers' names.

Now you do it with your life. Don't judge yourself. For some reason, our ego doesn't want us to connect with this part of ourselves, so it can be hard to put those critical voices aside. You know, the voices that say, "Oh, that's stupid" and "Oh, that's too simple" and "What a cliché" and "Look at all the times that isn't true." Acknowledge that voice, thank it for trying to keep you safe, and then continue to explore your experiences.

Ask yourself this: If you were at a restaurant sitting in a booth having a quick bite to eat and there were two people who you could overhear talking about you, what is *the* absolute worst thing they could say about you? I don't mean something that makes you cringe a bit; I mean that horrible thing that would make you want to throw up. *That* is tied to your *Hell Yeah!*

For me, I would be mortified if someone told me I didn't give value. They could say I wasn't the best painter; they didn't like my logo or website; or I didn't have good ideas and wasn't a good writer; they could even say I didn't have the best staff. Yes, all those things would *suck*, but none of those things would make me want to throw up like someone believing I'd ripped them off, wasted their time or money, or didn't care about their experience.

This is going to be different for different people, obviously. A violin maker (she would be called a luthier—I had to look that up) might not care much about customer service. Possibly, to her, clients are an inconvenience and a necessary evil, since they allow her to continue making violins. If she was in that restaurant and heard someone say that she made terrible-sounding violins that might crush her. She might not care if her violins are not the prettiest or the cheapest (in her case they would *not* be the cheapest) or if people thought she was a temperamental bitch, but if they didn't like the sound of her violins, that would be the worst thing ever. Making the best sounding violin is her *Hell Yeah!* and *everything* she does is geared to that focus: her education, her company's marketing, her community contribution, etc.

Explore for your own Hell Yeah! and then embrace it and use it to make all kinds of things in your life better.

Give me a high five and repeat after me. *Hell Yeah!*

Domino Thinking

As a way of exploring this concept of having a *Hell Yeah!* vision, take this opportunity to brainstorm what the *Hell Yeah!* might be for a business you have had contact with. Sometimes it is easier to look at someone else's practice and see how vision works, and then apply the same logic to your business.

I go to a hot yoga studio and I have had three less-than-stellar experiences regarding their customer service.

I was one of their first clients when they opened. I used to go five to six times a week and always at the same time, 9 a.m. If I had work come up, I would call as soon as I could so that someone else could take my spot in the class. Sometimes I would be the only who showed up for class and the owner would ask me if she could cancel the class. I always said yes.

Then the owner hired a front desk woman who implemented a new system. If a person didn't give nine hours of notice, they would lose a day off their monthly membership or their punch card. I couldn't always give that much notice, as sometimes I would find out at 7 a.m. if staff were sick and I had to take someone's place. I asked the yoga studio if there was another way. They said no. I ended up quitting. (I have a really hard time doing business with companies when I don't agree with or understand their policies.)

A year or two later, I bumped into the owner and she said she always felt bad about what happened and gave me a two-month pass for free to come back. They had a new, bigger studio and she said last-minute cancellations wouldn't be a problem any more. I was really happy about that and went to give them another go.

Three weeks in I got horribly sick with strep throat and asked to put the second month of the pass on hold. They said no. I quit again.

Alas, I really love hot yoga, so I am reluctantly now a member again, and I am confused about what they stand for. It's certainly not abundance (regardless of how much their instructors talk about abundance) and it's not about win-win (clearly) and they still have rules and restrictions that don't make a lot of sense. I hear them talking to other members with the same lack of care. I've talked with people in the community who have left their studio because of similar reasons. On the one hand they are contributing to charities but underneath they are falling short when handling their customers that keep them in business. Is it enough that they are doing good in one area but totally dropping the ball in another? I don't think so.

I go because they are the only place in town offering that type of yoga, but I go with a twinge of resentment every time. It's not very namaste-ish of me.

What does their vision seem to be to you?

What do you think it could be? (Let's just pretend you are all-knowing and your answer is the one we will go with.)

How do you think their policies could better align with that vision?

What are your feelings about this studio?

What businesses do you deal with that leave you feeling like this?

Do people feel this way about you and your business?

Think about this: How does what you think about this situation apply in some way to your business? Come up with two ideas of when you have rules that don't make sense.

Chapter 5

GET IN BED WITH
YOUR CUSTOMERS

"If you are an asshole, there's a pretty good chance your customers are going to be too."
— **Tanya**, my friend for long time

When I say "get in bed with your customers," I trust you know I don't mean you should all become prostitutes. I am talking about that time you spend with someone getting to know them before you jump in the sack—before you do business with them. Why is this important? Because you need your customers more than they need you. Unless you own the *only* food or water source, you need them more.

Why You Need Your Customers

This may sound like an elementary question: Why do you need your customers? Of course we need customers! But have you really thought about them further than the idea of you needing to sell your service or product? Would you have a relationship with someone who didn't care about you? Do you think you would be able to tell if someone didn't care about you? Newsflash: Your customers know if you care about them or not—and they know whether you think about them or not.

Yes, marketing experts say to "know your demographic." That makes sense. I don't hear a lot of them talking about how your customers help propel your *Hell Yeah!* forward. How you need to understand how your *Hell Yeah!* relates to them and how they relate to it. When you get your customers behind your mission, there will be no stopping you or your important *Hell Yeah!* (Just ask Apple. That company is probably the best example of fostering loyal customers.)

I ask you to really spend time understanding why you need your customers—beyond the fact that you have bills to pay. The time you spend with this question will strengthen your appreciation of them, which in turn, will build your relationships with them.

"Customer service" is one of those terms that companies toss around, but only a few companies seem to really understand. Be one of the companies that understands.

What Your Customers Are *Not*

Your customers are *not* an inconvenience, even though sometimes they may seem that way. Your customers are not always right, even though sometimes they may think so. When we understand what customers truly are *not*, we can better understand what they are. Stay with me here.

If you have ten people in a room and you eliminate nine because they are *not* your customers, the one left will be your customer. Sometimes it is easier to eliminate than select.

Let's look at an example. Mike is in the weight-loss industry and his *Hell Yeah!* is helping women get back to their pre-pregnancy shape and size. He needs to get into the heads of people who are trying to get pregnant, who are pregnant, or who just had a baby.

Let's list what Mike's clients are not. It's safe to say they are not men. Pre-pubescent, menopausal and post-menopausal women are also out.

Next, Mike can consider the financial situation of whom he's looking to work with. If his focus is on those who can't typically afford help in this area, then he eliminates all those above a certain income bracket. If Mike feels he won't be effective working with people who can't afford groceries, then he will eliminate those who are *below* a certain income bracket.

After eliminating based on gender, age, and income, what other variables will Mike want to use to eliminate customers? Geography? Employment? Are they interested in having children? Are they planning? Are they in the process or finished being pregnant? He keeps picking away at the stats until he finds his ideal group, and then, by default, he will know who his client *is* because he knows who they are not.

Once you have identified your customer, you might want to consider what type of customer your business will attract in terms of longevity.

Not all businesses require or need repeat clients. Take, for example, a company that builds houses. Chances are, they are only going to get a client once, and then they will need to find a new client. How they treat that client and the money they put in to retaining that client has a different value for the business than a gym has, because a gym wants their clients to keep renewing their memberships every year.

Is your client a one-off? Are they someone who will need a job done once, but appreciate it and then recommend you to others? Or are you attracting a lifer?

The Benefits of Having Good Customers

Well, this part is easy. No customers, no money! The benefit of having *good* customers however, is undervalued. Even if, in the section above, you determined that you have one-time-only customers, there is still word of mouth to consider. We all know that word of mouth is better than any advertising money can buy.

Let's go back to Apple. Their customers are die-hard fans. I know I am. I won't even look at another computer when I'm in the market. I've been using Macs since 2005. I was nervous about switching, but a friend of mine who I thought was super cool and was always on the cutting-edge used one, and convinced me it was the way to go.

An hour into using my new laptop I was sold. Since 2005 I have converted almost everyone I know. I feel a kindred-ness with other Mac users and an appreciation for the service and support I receive. By caring about their clients, Apple doesn't have to have all the groovy ads they have (but I am glad they do, because they *are* groovy), because their loyal users sell their products for them. Their ads have become our authority source, rather than the company's source of clients.

Apple fans do the selling for them. How do you get your customers to do your selling for you?

The Problem with Having Bad Customers

We cannot measure the damage an angry client does, nor can we eradicate it. The really crazy part is that people don't remember where they heard a *bad* review. If you have a crazy client, you may tell yourself that his friends must be crazy too, so you don't want them for clients either. Or that his friends know he is an asshole and so won't believe what he says when he gives your business a bad review. In theory, that makes sense. Is it a good call to think that way? Nope, not so much. His crazy-ass friends are going to help him spread the word, and his friends who aren't crazy but know he is will still take in the information. Then, on a random Tuesday six months down the road, your company name will come up and they will say, "Oh, I heard something bad about them. I don't remember what it was or who told me, but apparently they do terrible work." And so it goes. They tell two people, who tell two people, and so on and so on.

The best thing you can do is screen your clients to avoid the crazy ones. If one slips through the cracks and you think they are crazy, you can let them come up with a reason for leaving you. Let it be their idea about why your business isn't right for them, before you do any work for them. People leave much more easily and are happier when they think it's their choice.

Not everyone is a good potential client, nor should they be. A client who will not contribute to spreading your *Hell Yeah!* will deplete you financially and emotionally. Time-sucking-clients-from-hell causes you to neglect your really great clients.

The other choice for weeding out the crazies is to have such great customer service policies that it's really hard to get mad at you. Let me give you two examples.

First, Bruce Poon Tip, the founder and brilliant brain behind G Adventures, has redefined sustainable travel and the customer experience. I have travelled with G Adventures twice, once to southern Africa and once to Cambodia, and I recommend them to everyone. Their awareness of great customer service includes doing things like offering a lifetime deposit policy where, if you put a deposit on a trip and are unable to make it, then—no questions asked—you can transfer your deposit and use it at a later date on a different trip. Why can't all companies do things like that? It creates such great loyalty. Who can feel animosity toward a company like that? (You can check them out at www.gadventures.com.)

The second example is a local company. Linda owns a tanning salon called Divine Glow (www.divineglow.ca). I keep telling that her she needs to run customer service workshops. I have been going to her for years. She is known in the community as the go-to place for tanning (I live in rainy British Columbia). Linda supports local events and she tries to always say yes. I use the monthly package, but if something comes up and I can't make the last two weeks of a month, Linda will put it on hold. If I buy a package and realize I am not going to use it, I can transfer it to a later month. If I stop in without an appointment (which I do frequently), she never makes me feel bad and does her best to accommodate me. I moved further away from her shop, but I still go to her salon. If I see someone standing outside her shop looking at her advertised pricing, I talk him or her into going in. I sing Linda's praises. If I ever hear of anyone wanting to tan, I tell him or her about her shop. I love her. Her business has won Best of the City awards for the last three years for a reason. Compare my experience with Linda and her business to the Domino Thinking example in Chapter 4 about the yoga studio: I am always going to be looking for a better yoga studio; I will never leave Linda.

Having great policies doesn't eliminate angry clients -people will still be people- but it reduces the number and frequency.

What are your policies and how could you change them to offer better customer service? Think about it. What does Linda have to lose by letting me put a package on hold? What does G Adventures lose by honoring my deposit? Nothing. What policies do you have that exist just because "that's the way we do it" and not "that's what is best for the client, and what do we have to lose?"

How to Get in Bed with Your Customer

Think of your customer as the person on the other side of the chessboard. I pick chess as an example because I like it, not because I think this is a complicated relationship. Have you ever tried to play chess by yourself? I don't mean on the computer where the computer is playing your opponent's moves. I mean playing a white piece, spinning the board, and playing a black piece, and so on. My suggestion is for you to play by yourself for a while, if for no other reason than it gives you a constant perspective switch to "the other side."

You make a move, and the beauty of it is that you get to play the next piece *inside* the brain of your opponent because *you* are your opponent. Relating this to customer service, once you have considered your moves from the opponent's chair, from your customer's perspective, you can understand what your moves feel like to them and how you are going to respond to them. *Now* you can invite your customer to play with you, which is not to say you shouldn't play the odd game by yourself to make sure you still like your moves, but once you understand how you show up and participate in the game of customer service, you will be able to serve your customer more effectively.

Let's do an exercise. Grab a pen and paper and draw a line down the middle of the page.

Remember a restaurant experience you had. Write down all of your points of contact with the staff from beginning to end in one column.

Now really think about whether you have listed all the points of contact. Look at your first point. Could you go back a step further? Was the first point of contact walking in the door and being greeted? What about when you were in the parking lot? Or when you first thought you might want to go out for dinner? Maybe when you asked a friend about their experience? How about when you checked the restaurant's website to check their hours?

This list can really grow. See how many points you can come up with. When you feel you have exhausted the list, write in the second column how you want to *feel* at each point of contact. Do you want to feel welcomed? Like it's a clean environment? Confident about your choice or the recommendation from your friends? Do you want to go back?

Notice that not once have you commented on how you want the *owner* to feel. As customers, we don't really care about the owners. We care about our *experience*.

Next, beside each point of contact mark which experiences you can control. When you hit a contact point that you cannot control, see if the next point of contact provides you with an opportunity to make up for it. There is nothing worse than having to wait for a table and then also getting unfriendly service. If a restaurant is making you wait, they should make sure the service is outstanding. Then customers are more likely to forgive them for the wait.

We have a Cactus Club in town and the parking *sucks*. When I walk up to the restaurant and someone holds the door open for me and welcomes me inside, I forget how much I hate their parking lot. I soon remember that I hate their propensity for scantily clad women in heels, but then remind myself that, as a female, I am not their target audience. Then I remember that I love their lettuce wraps. So it goes, back and forth. Love them, hate them; it makes for a confusing relationship for me.

This is where a business' *Hell Yeah!* is so very important. The customer service—and the branding—is embedded in your *Hell Yeah!* Think about your business. What are your points of contact with your customers? How do *they* want to feel?

What can you control about their experience and what can't you control? Why are your policies in place? This can be really tough to sort out, because you are *inside* your business and so you know it from your perspective. You have to get *outside* your business in order to get "in bed with," your customers needs and know what makes them tick.

Gear all your energy towards those who need your vision. Understand who they are, what they need, and how they are going to feel about their experiences with you.

Domino Thinking

I had a client who dealt in packaging. He was in contact with garbologists (yes, there is such a thing). He told me that there are two very different camps in garbology: those who think garbage is bad and all things should be recycled, and those who think recycling is not really the best option. I live on a tree-hugging island, so I was more fascinated with those who didn't agree with recycling than with those who promoted it. A few of the things I retained from that conversation were:

- The paper we recycle is okay, but no one questions whether the ink used for branding is biodegradable. Often, it's not, and because this new paper breaks down so quickly, that ink gets into our ground and our water sources quickly.
- Humans like to wait until something hits a critical mass and then our creativity kicks in and we do something really amazing, like maybe actually using less in the first place, or repurposing "garbage" items into building

supplies, or something like that. Recycling has slowed down the accumulation of garbage, thus slowing down our ingenuity.

Whether those issues are real or imagined, that conversation got me thinking about how we take such movements for granted because we think that smarter people than us are telling us that recycling is good. We forget or don't know that recycling is a gazillion-dollar industry. We don't think about things like being at the grocery store and putting a fresh chicken package in our cloth bag and then putting the bags on dirty counters and not washing the cloth bag often, or ever, and thus spreading germs.

What are you accepting as truth that needs to be questioned? This is important to think about. Not so long ago, we denied climate change and blindly threw everything out rather than reusing or recycling. Now are we blindly following the recycling movement?

Think about this: How does what you think about this situation apply in some way to your business? Come up with two ideas about what you take for granted.

Chapter 6

LET YOUR STAFF BE KICK-ASS

"A well cultivated culture is contagious."
— **Audrea Hooper**—Zappo's thought-provoking
Head of Fungineering

The relationship between owners and staff is intriguing. Each party has different needs and yet they are reliant on each other. There seems to be an understanding that the roles are different, but we never really seem to talk about it. How would the dynamic change if we talked about our respective roles with each other more often and more deeply?

Why You Need to Let Your Staff Be Kick-Ass

It's not enough to let your staff kick ass, you must encourage them to *be* kick-ass.

Letting them implies that they are being managed or that they need permission, while *being* is a state of existence. You do not just want them to be kick-ass at work; you want them to be kick-ass in *life*.

Let's face it, when people are inspired, they are more fun to be around and they care more about what they are doing. Your staff stands between you and your customers and your staff are an intricate and vital part of your business. It's up to you to define what that looks like.

It's not enough to just *have* staff, you must *engage* them. Staff who are only putting in time are a dangerous waste of *your* time, money, and reputation.

Have you ever gone into a store and really wanted to buy something, yet the staff could care less that you're there? If you are anything like me, you turn around and walk out. I do not want to support a business that doesn't *want* to engage their staff or where I matter so little that they don't *need* to engage their staff.

Conversely, have you been in a store and had an experience that made you want to write to the owner of the company to say that their staff member was tremendous? What a different experience. *Hell yeah!* I want to support a business when they obviously care how they interact with me.

At the beginning of this chapter I quoted Audrea, who works at Zappos. I met her at a workshop in Vegas and she spoke about moving from a company where the staff was grumpy to

Zappos where everyone is nice and happy and loves their jobs. She told me that, at first, she was suspicious of the new work atmosphere. When she first started at Zappos, there was a co-worker who would say, "Hi! How are you today?" or "Isn't it a beautiful day?" or "It's so nice to see you"—*every single day*. At first, Audrea thought the woman was an unusually happy staff member, but she soon noticed that everyone was like that. It was such a different environment, and that was their *everyday* attitude. The kicker is that it took her a long time to trust her new environment.

Why is it that we think working has to be drudgery, that if we are having fun and being friendly it's not really work and we are not taking it seriously enough? Is it our Puritan influence of nose to the grindstone?

If we spend an average of 40 hours a week working, that's 2080 hours a year. We only have 8544 hours in a year. Factor in time spent in transit—let's call that 1.5 hours a day being potentially unhappy at the other drivers or delays in the trains, and time getting ready for work—let's call that 45 minutes a day. Good grief. Do the math: 2080 hours of work + 390 hours getting to and from work + 195 hours getting ready for work = 2665 hours a year on work. That is a fuck of a long time to be unhappy.

Yet we accept this. So much so, that if we are lucky enough to land in a job where the staff is happy—we don't trust it. That is so backwards.

Think about housework. When you have tunes blasting and you're dancing around while cleaning up the house, do you feel good and productive? Contrast that to when your in-laws are coming over and you are not looking forward to it because you know your lovely Ma-in-law is going to find *something* to complain about, no matter what, so why even bother trying to make things look good. That is the difference between staff who like coming to work and those who don't. The difference between enjoying doing a job you like or dreading it. Staff who are getting the work done without someone looking over their shoulder, counting their mistakes, and micromanaging are going to be happier, feel trusted, and ultimately do much better at their jobs.

It is our responsibility to be happy and, yes, that means being happy at our jobs too. Why can't we enjoy ourselves? We can't control how other people run their companies or departments, but we sure as hell can control how we run ours. The way to do that is to *engage with our staff*. We can trust that we hired them because we thought they would be good for our *Hell Yeah*! So *let them be good*. Let them be great!

When our staff are on our side, they act as extensions of ourselves. When we trust them to do what is best for the business, we are trusting them to do what is best for us. That is huge! It's a beautiful thing to be on the same page as our crew. When your staff are kicking ass it allows you to focus on ways to advance your company, or to take a trip, or to deal with a family emergency.

It moves the relationship from one of babysitting to collaboration.

What Happens When Your Staff Are Not Allowed to Be Kick-Ass

When staff is not allowed to kick-ass, they are boring, uninspired, and harmful to your business. When they do not know, share, or embrace your *Hell Yeah!*, they start to work for your competition. By not serving your customers they are sending them to the businesses next door who *do* care about their customers. The messed up part is that you are paying your staff to alienate your clients, and *that* is insanity.

If you prohibit your staff from being kick-ass, you are telling them you don't trust them and they are not smart enough to make decisions. Yes, there is a hierarchy in business, but when your staff is on board with your vision they are working *with* you not against you.

Hiring staff and then micromanaging them begs the question of why you hired them in the first place. Just get rid of them and do their jobs yourself. If you *want* to micromanage, then have a business where you don't have to have staff.

The Benefits of Kick-Ass Staff

As discussed earlier, when your staff feel trusted and are empowered, they are on your side, they get your vision, and they will go out of their way all of the time to contribute.

Let's go back to that example of you cleaning your house for your Ma-in-law's visit. How would that experience be different if you knew she was going to be thrilled with your efforts? If the two of you could talk about cool tricks to make cleaning easier or more enjoyable. Maybe she would let you in on a family secret about how baking soda and vinegar will unclog your drain, or you will tell her about a great article you read about how toothpaste will polish your kitchen taps. Sometimes, when she knows you are tired, she will come over and surprise you by scrubbing your bathroom, or you will pick up extra bathtub cleaner when you see that it's on sale and give one to her.

I don't know about you, but I felt good just reading that paragraph. I want a Ma-in-law I can be that way with. Do you see that if your staff is excited to have you come around, then they will look for things to show you and they will contribute, but if they are anxious about seeing you they are not going to perform as well?

If we bring a collaborative attitude into our businesses and extend that philosophy to our staff, they will be happy to come to work, they will feel part of the process, and they will make choices that benefit everyone—because the success or failure of the company becomes their own success or failure. They bring who they are as people into the workplace, and who they are is the reason you hired them in the first place.

There was a woman who worked for me once as a painter and she would submit her time sheet and say things like, "On that day I only worked eight hours, but I put in for ten hours because I hauled butt and got a huge amount of work done." At first, I was a bit apprehensive, but I agreed to pay her for the ten hours. It turned out that she began to *also* say on certain days that she was really tired and, although she had been on the job for eight hours, she really had only worked six hours—and she would adjust her time sheet that way too. When I trusted her to charge me for the hours she actually worked, she was happier, she thought about her job differently, and she never ripped me off on hours.

How to Get Your Staff to Be Kick-Ass

Now that you are becoming more clear about your *Hell Yeah!*, you get to share it with your staff. Have meetings about it, share ideas on how to implement it, make your workspace unique and personalized.

Why not give your staff cool titles based on their skill sets? Sue is amazing with lists and getting organized and always makes sure things get done. Call her Ms. Do List. Brad is super logical and calm in a crisis, so call him Spock. Have fun with them.

Have you seen the movie *Deadpool*? It's vulgar and obnoxious and funny and I loved it! The opening credits didn't list the cast and crew by name, but rather the director was referred to as "An Overpaid Tool" and the writers were "The Real Heroes Here" and Ryan Reynolds was listed as "God's Perfect Idiot." Granted, those titles were a bit of a roast, but I am hoping you get the point. *Have fun*. People love nicknames, especially when they are well thought out, well earned, play up their positive aspects, and given with affection.

Empowering your staff is one of the ways to keep them on your team. Empowering is not just a popular word these days. Take a moment and *think* about what *empower* means? The dictionary defines empower as giving full power to someone. How can you empower your staff?

I spoke once to a man who worked for Westjet, a Canadian airline company with a reputation for being caring. He worked in the call center and told me with pride how the company empowered him to make decisions. He told me about a woman who called up, frantic because a loved one was in the hospital and she needed to reach him. There was limited space on the flight, but the man complimented her a return flight, even though they were expensive due to the last-minute booking. He felt very good about this choice and most likely won a loyal customer for life. He only did that once throughout his career though, because he had respect for Westjet and for the trust they put in him and he didn't want to abuse it.

Mindvalley is a company created by Vishen Lakhiani. He believes so strongly that we are the sum of the five people we hang out with most that he makes an effort to up the game with his staff. He gets them in front of the best of the best to allow them to raise their own standards. Every year he takes his staff to an event he creates just for them called A-Fest. Maybe you can't afford such an extreme event, but perhaps there are team-building things you can do. Bungee-jumping? Camping trip? Cooking class?

We can do whatever we want to with our businesses, which means we can get our staff on board. We do not have to be restricted by the way things are "always done." There is some validity in using what's "tried, tested, and true," but isn't there a higher level we can aspire to? We can include our staff in the journey so that our ways of doing business become the new tried, trusted, and true.

Domino Thinking

Here is an opportunity for you to consider some of your beliefs and apply some critical thinking to them.

Are you pro-life or pro-choice? (Don't worry, this is not a test and there is no wrong answer.)

Let's take a moment and think about why you take the stance you take on this topic. Is it from personal experience? Because of your religion? Your family values? Research you read?

Now let's think about what you think about the people involved. Are they good or bad? What is their motive for doing what they are doing? What do you think about the doctors? The women? The fetus? The fathers?

Now, let's look at the experiences. Why is she getting an abortion? Do you think that a politician aggressively opposing abortion has considered this question? What does getting an abortion feel like physically? What does it feel like mentally? What are the aftereffects? Why do doctors opt to do this procedure?

Now, step back and go through those questions again from the other side of the argument, from the position of pro-choice.

If you believe in pro-life and abortion becomes illegal, what happens to a woman or the doctor if she gets an abortion? She *will* get an abortion—history has shown that. It would be considered premeditated murder and the doctor would be an accessory to first-degree murder and they could both be sentenced to life and, in some states, the death penalty.

How do you feel about that?

Think of the most extreme situation a woman could endure that would cause her to seek out an abortion. Perhaps she is 13 years old and is raped. Can she have an abortion? Is it okay to pick and choose who gets charged and sentenced and who gets to be an exception?

Conversely, if you believe in pro-choice, that people have the right to do what they want with their own body, does that mean you believe in the right to die with dignity? How about the rights of homosexuals? What about suicide? How about choosing drug addiction? At what point does a person no longer get to choose?

I invite you to think about these issues and talk to your friends about them. Then apply this way of thinking deeply to other things you believe in.

Remember that critical thinking is going to change the world and that your part is to *think* and to challenge others to think, to seek clarity and education—without judgement.

Think about this: How does what you think about this situation apply in some way to your business? Come up with two ideas of how you bring your belief systems to work, or the belief systems you have about work.

Chapter 7
GIVE LOVE
WHERE YOU LIVE

"Give yourself the gift of community; interact, be present and become a part of people's lives."
— **Gina Best**—the toughest, kindest woman I know.

We do not live our life in a plastic bubble, nor do we live life completely independent of other people. We may think we are an island and we don't need anyone's help, but we rely on people and need their help all the time. When we recognize our inter-reliance we can begin to understand how we can make a *Hell Yeah!* impact.

Why You Need to Give Love Where You Live

We tap into other people all the time. We rely on our doctors to take care of us; we rely on the server to bring us food from the kitchen that won't make us sick. We rely on the other drivers on the road to not drive into us, and on those who operate the subway to get us to our destination without going headlong into another train. We are all connected.

If we are all connected, then why *wouldn't* we care about the kids selling lemonade at the ends of their driveways? Those children will one day grow up and, when they do, they are going to be the people running our government, or running the nursing homes our children put us in. So support them and encourage them.

What about the veteran on the street who went to war for his country and came back messed up psychologically and is trying to live with the horrible things he saw and did? We owe it to him to see him as a person. He is one of us. He matters. We all matter.

Giving is good for your soul. It's that simple. And if it's good for your soul, it's good for your business. There is suffering all around us—people trying to do better, be better. When we help them with that, we validate their efforts. Sometimes, for some people, getting out of bed takes so much effort that it's elusive. There are all kinds of people who could use some help.

It's not just the giving that counts; it's building up the dreams of the people around you in the place where you live. When you can help your fellow person, they can help others and the world becomes better.

It is only by the grace of God, or whoever you believe in, that you are in your shoes and not theirs. You got a good set of parents or a good education. The right person at the right time said something to you that made you believe in yourself. You were born on a lucky Tuesday when the planets were lined up. We don't really know why we are *here* and not *there*. When we stop and give, it offers us a chance to take *in* that moment and be grateful. That is the gift we get out of giving, not the pat on the back, the tax receipt, or the award. *We get to be grateful.*

When we are able to give to someone else with awareness, we are also giving a gift to ourselves. It is impossible to give to another person and get hurt in the process. The hurt comes from not having a realization of *ourselves* before we give, such that our giving has ulterior motives or conditions. So start by knowing why you are giving—and then give freely.

When Giving Love Is Not Really Giving Love

When you are not giving love with awareness, you are not helping; you only think you are.

Consider this. Dave and his staff decide to create a gift basket for a family at Christmas. Is this helping or not? They feel good about doing it. They sound good to their friends. It eases their guilt about their big Christmas vacation coming up and their lavish gifts for each other. But are they *really* thinking about the family and what that family *really* needs?

Granted, some aid programs are better thought-out than others, but for the sake of this growth exercise, let's dig further. What is the application process the families go through to try to get a basket? Why do the families need a gift basket? Do they need something else, but the gift basket is the only thing available to them, because some arbitrary group decided giving it was necessary? Would they be better served with help getting a job? Or with getting a ride to the hospital if they are on medical disability? What about giving a bursary for their child to go to college? Maybe none of that sounds as appealing as, "Oh, look at me. I did something for a family I don't even know." We may not say that verbatim, but we may be feeling it. Do Dave and his staff understand what they are contributing to beyond the act of giving the basket?

When we don't give with awareness, we may cause more of the same problems. If a family always gets presents at Christmas from strangers, why would they do anything differently but expect other people outside the family to put a gift basket under their tree? If a person becomes accustomed to going to a food bank, will they ever learn how to feed themselves? If you think it through and see that the value of the gift is for the recipient more than it is for you, then go hard, give until your heart is content. Until you know as much as you can about your own process with giving, you are not giving with love.

In the past, I belonged to a networking group. It was our mandate that we donated all our unused membership dues to a local charity. It was close to Christmas and we were tasked to make a decision. Our first mistake was that there was no *Hell Yeah!* for our group. The second mistake was that when the decision was made to donate the money there was no mandate set out about where it would go or how to do it. The third mistake was that we didn't have any guidance about donating during the Christmas season and we were at an emotional time of year.

What do you think—do you think we ended up making a good choice? Probably not. Our decision was to donate the money to a home for battered women. Did it help? Yes. Does that make it a good choice that was representative of our group? No.

If we were a group of women who had come from abusive relationships, then it would have been a perfect choice, one that was aligned with our collective *Hell Yeah!* But we were a group of entrepreneurs from a hodgepodge of backgrounds. I wonder if we would have made a different decision if it hadn't been Christmas. Most likely.

What do you think would have been a good fit for our gift of money?

The Benefits of Giving Love Where You Live

Take time out of thinking about your own world and your own problems and think about someone else's pain. Let's face it; we don't often give to a charity that is not trying to alleviate pain. When we put some love into the world, it multiplies. Aren't your days easier when people show you kindness? Don't you feel a little bit better when you buy coffee for the person behind you in the drive-through or hold the door open for a mom with a stroller?

Engaged businesses make for healthy communities. I don't know what it is like where you live, but I am constantly being asked for money. There are a lot of groups and individuals in need.

This is where your *Hell Yeah!* comes in handy. If your *Hell Yeah!* is to help people get fit, then how about directing the money you have set aside in your business to contribute toward organizations in your community that support fitness? That is *in line* with your vision. If you give to the local animal shelter instead, that doesn't make as much sense, and it certainly won't make sense to your customers. This is not to say you can't incorporate animal shelters into your giving strategy, but do it in a way that makes sense for your *Hell Yeah!*

Like everything else in your business, it helps to be consistent. This is why you created your *Hell Yeah!*—you want your customers and your staff to be clear. Does it not stand to reason that you want your community to be clear too? It's all one big package. In my experience, most businesses contribute randomly and without a plan. This weakens their vision.

When I go into my doctor's office and I see a fundraiser flyer for NanGo Grannies, a branch of the Stephen Lewis Foundation that has grandmothers in North America helping grandmothers in Sub Sahara Africa to bring up their AIDS-orphaned grandchildren, I feel good about contributing, because I know it is in alignment with my doctor's values, and I value her. If her fundraiser was for a local dance school raising funds to go to Seattle for a dance competition, I may not contribute, because that seems out of alignment with what my doctor does in her business. If she does things that don't make sense, I lose a bit of trust.

The point is not that my doctor shouldn't contribute to a dance competition. It's that it would require some explanation. If I knew she had always wanted to be a dancer, but she'd had a bad car accident that ended her dream and, through her rehabilitation, she had such a profound experience with her medical care that she decided to become a doctor, then the fundraising would make a lot more sense and I would support it. It would help for her to have all of her fundraising efforts point in that direction so there was a cohesive theme.

The other beautiful thing about having a theme is that it allows you promote what you support. When you do that two things happen. First, you further share your *Hell Yeah!* with your customers and staff. Second, you stop getting caught off guard with other causes. You can simply say, "I appreciate that you are excited about your cause and I wish you all the best, but it doesn't fall into the cause I support." This allows you to be clear, not waste time, and not get caught up in the guilt of saying no. There is *nothing* better than a clear vision.

The Problem with Not Giving Love

When we don't give love in our communities we can't really claim to be part of the community; we are simply taking up space. This always reminds me of the Garth Brooks song "Standing Outside the Fire" which has the message that it might be cool to stand outside the fire, but life is not truly lived unless you are inside the fire. So get involved. Show compassion. Make a difference. Take a chance. Be that person in someone's life who they look back on and say, "There was this guy who made a difference" or "A woman heard me and helped me." Get involved in a way that fits for you and is aligned with your *Hell Yeah!*

If we don't jump into our communities, we withhold the gifts we have been given. When we withhold those gifts we are being selfish. You may not think your gift of yourself is significant enough to anyone, but it is. You do what you do best with ease and grace and rarely think about it as anything special. To someone who doesn't have your gifts, what you do is magic. When you don't support your community, you don't grow at the same rate as someone who does.

What would your community look like if no one gave anything? Would your children get to play sports if no one volunteered to coach? Would the seniors in your community lose the young people who volunteer and visit with them and remind them that they matter and that their stories and wisdom are worth sharing? What about the neighbour who shovels your sidewalk just because he is already doing his and he knows you are busy? How do you feel about those things, those gifts? Do they matter? Damn right they matter. Don't you feel a little bit better about the world when someone does something nice for you or gives you a gift of some kind? Don't you feel uplifted if you'd been having a bad day? Why would you want to withhold that from someone in your community?

The Best Way to Give Love Where You Live

The best way to contribute is by doing something you love doing in a way that fuels you, so that you feel energized and not drained and resentful about giving.

So think about it. What is your *Hell Yeah!*? What is the best way you feel when you are delivering it? If you are a life coach, what about donating two hours a month to people who can't afford what you are offering. If you specialize in digital media, find a group that fits with your vision and help them out. If you don't want to offer your services, then offer your hobby to something that is aligned with your *Hell Yeah!* Maybe you are a life coach but don't feel right about giving coaching, but since you focus on healthy lifestyle issues in your coaching maybe it would make sense to do gardening at community gardens and teach people how to garden.

Let's take this to a bigger scale. You have a company with 600 employees. How do you contribute? Maybe you have considered your vision and feel that youth in sports is your focus. Get that vision on your website and let sports teams in the area know you are willing to sponsor them. But don't stop there. Do an incentive in your company for people to get involved in supporting youth in sports and feature them on your website page. Get excited about the changes you are making and promote it. Let everyone see. Raise the bar for other companies. Challenge them to do the same.

Do you even know what community groups fall into your business mandate topic? Or do you give on a whim? Do you see how aligning your *Hell Yeah!* with your customers and again with your staff and again with your community gives you a stronger position and a better way to make a positive impact?

Domino Thinking

What policies do you have in place that make no sense yet you are asking people to accommodate them?

A few years ago, a client called me up and asked me for a copy of her invoice. The conversation went like this:

Her: Can you send me a copy of my invoice

Me: You would have been emailed one. Did you not receive it?

Her: Yes, but I want a hard copy

Me: Okay, you can print it.

Her: No, I am on a paperless system—it's better for the environment.

Me: So you want *me* to print it and mail it.

Her: Yes.

Me: How does this make sense? Whether you print it or I print it, that equals the same thing right—a hard copy invoice?

Her: Right, except I am using paperless system and can't print it.

Me: So because you are paperless, you want me to print it, put it in an envelope, drive in to the store in a vehicle that uses fossil fuels so I can buy a stamp and mail it. You want that piece of mail, which went through all the many steps—including postal workers driving, lights on in the warehouse, machines working for sorting, etc.—and then have it driven to a station in your area so that another vehicle can drive it to your mailbox? All because you are using a paperless system?

Her: Yes.

Me: How is that better for the environment?

Now, maybe she just didn't have a printer. If so, fair enough. But it would still have made more sense for her to put the invoice I'd sent her onto a thumb drive and walk to her local Staples and print it than for her to try to get me to mail it.

How many things do we do that we think are better but actually are making things worse?

Start looking at what you do and what the people around you do and see if what they are doing really is the "better" way, and then maybe start a conversation.

Think about this: How does what you think about this situation apply in some way to your business? Come up with two ideas of policies you may not have thought through.

Chapter 8
THE WORLD NEEDS YOU

"Push yourself out of your comfort zones—even to the edges—because that is where we learn who we are. That is where we face our demons and rise to new heights of awareness. That is when we start living!"

— **Todd Sinclair**—the best tour leader ever

What is going on in the world affects you, like it or not. We are being affected by all kinds of things all the time. We are affected by terrorism, by global warming, by elections, by global warming. We are not operating in isolation anymore. Everything is in our own backyard.

We think that the world is a big place, but access to computers and affordable travel has shrunk the globe. We are now more affected by, and more able to affect, the world than ever before in history.

This is good news! What this means for your business—and beyond—is that you can have a far-reaching impact. With some thinking, you can see how you can change the world for the better. This may seem daunting, but in many ways you will impact the world just by going about your life with awareness and trying to raise awareness in others. Then, when every once in a while you are faced with a concrete way you can create change, you will be ready to act on it.

Why the World Needs You

You already understand the need to think critically. You may not always be applying it, but you know how crucial the process is. You know that it starts with you, moves on to affect your customers, staff, and community. Ultimately, it cannot help but affect the world around you.

By changing how you think, you change everyone around you. Your customers will grow to expect more from other companies. Your staff will not only excel in their positions with your company, they will also excel in their own lives, thus affecting the people they connect with. Your community will appreciate your contribution and will see themselves differently through you. These people will, in turn, impact the world around them.

Yes, you are only one person, but if you think about the domino effect of your actions you will no longer be able to underestimate your importance.

Let's look back at Bruce Poon Tip, the founder of G Adventures, who I mentioned in Chapter 5. I adore what he does and because I am a lover of travel, he has stolen my heart. He is an amazing example of what one person can do. His vision changed him, his customers, his staff, his community, and the world, but he started out just wanting to change travel. He even went so far as to create his own charity.

One man.

One vision.

Massive change.

What the World Doesn't Need

The world doesn't need any more people imposing their will. You don't have to look far back in our history books to see the damage that has been done by thinking that *our* way or *my* way is *the* way.

Good intentions pave the road to hell. Ask any culture that has been divided by war or religion. I don't know what it is about humanity that makes some of us feel superior to others to the point of assuming they know what is better for everyone, but good intentions do not equal *right*.

I once heard a woman speak who was asking for connections with people who live in China so she could go and speak to women there about how they could "have more." I couldn't help but wonder if she fully understood what women's lives were like in China. I certainly didn't. Did those women she was referring to want to change? Were they unhappy? And if they did want to hear her words, would that actually make their lives better or worse? Was she projecting her own idea of womanhood on another culture?

Afterward, I spoke with a friend whose wife is Chinese, because I wanted to hear his thoughts. He shook his head and laughed, saying that we white women had no idea what life was like for Chinese women. They may seem subservient, but they often rule their households, and those who rule the households rule the country. I have thought about that a lot since our discussion and it's changed how I think about other things I had been making assumptions about.

There may be a lot of things that are different between cultures, but being told what we want by someone else is universally offensive.

Just because we have a thought doesn't make it a right thought or one that fulfills a need. Sometimes the best thing to do is to *ask* people what they need. How many people do you know who decided what people needed and gave them based on that, and then wondered why their efforts were not effective? More importantly, are we causing damage by not really understanding their points of view?

When we ask people what they need, we risk losing that rush of altruism; that oh-I-just-solved-a-huge-problem-all-on-my-own feeling. Asking requires far more work, because we have to find the people we want to help and ask them what help looks like for them.

Consider the medical industry. They look at the issue of AIDS in Third World countries and may think that what people need is AIDS testing. But what if the women in some of those countries know that their husbands won't let them take an anti-retroviral, or what if they will be ostracized if they test positive? Is that a win for those women? Perhaps what would be more important to them is to not know they have AIDS, but to have a local well built so they don't have to walk endlessly for water as their health deteriorates.

But *damn*. It would feel better to be the big shot who cured someone of AIDS. But would it be better if it didn't make their life better?

The Benefits of Serving the World

More than likely, you are not the disadvantaged in your community. I am certain that if you are reading this book, you are not among the disadvantaged in the world. You could have been born into a culture where female circumcision is a way of life or where wearing a bomb strapped to your chest is considered a solution, but you weren't.

You were born where you are and you get to be the person who makes this world better for those who weren't as lucky. This does not mean fixing them. It means listening to what they say they need, then deciding if you can fulfill that need.

When you are part of building a better world, the focus moves off of you and onto humanity as a whole. If you have children or grandchildren or nieces or nephews, you get to know you are leaving them with a world that's a little bit better than when you found it. I know this can sound cliché, but really, what else do you have to do? You can go about running your business and making the world better, or you can go about running your business and making the world worse. It's your choice. Children and grandchild aside, we just *feel* better when we *do* better.

We are capable of horrific acts. We have destroyed other cultures because they are different than ours. We are hell-bent on destroying the environment. The absolutely beautiful thing is that we are also capable of tremendous acts of kindness and bravery. We have protected people who were being persecuted. We have taken huge steps to being inclusive. We have raised awareness about the environment. The reality is that a few years after we die, few people will really remember us. But if you make an impact on the world, *that* is remembered. Although people may not remember your name, you will have impacted them and you live through that. That will be your legacy.

When we see the world as an extension of ourselves and our legacy, we understand how vital our impact is. We see the domino effect of our actions. Now that you have started to think about the implications of your actions, you can no longer be oblivious to how much the world needs you.

Consider some of the amazing people who have had a positive impact. Gandhi showed the world there is a peaceful alternative. Muhammad Ali didn't just shape the world of boxing, he refused to go to war, he chose his own religion, and he was an advocate of freedom and equality.

You don't have to be Gandhi or Ali to make a difference. Every person I quoted at the beginnings of the chapters has made an impact on the world because they have made an impact on me. Think about that.

Do you have a version of Gandhi or Ali in your world—someone who had a big impact just by being themselves and wanting to help? I bet you do. That teacher who saw your brilliance? The coach who encouraged you even though you weren't really a great athlete? The boss who loved your ideas?

There is a really good chance they didn't even know they were impacting you. They were just being quintessentially themselves.

My son had a really good friend in high school who had a troubled home life. He used to come over and I would give him hell when he misbehaved. One day, I gave him and a couple of other boys, including my son, three rules:

1. If you are going to fight, fight to win. (I guess I figured they would think twice about fighting, because if they lost they would be in trouble.)
2. If you end up in jail, do not call me until morning. (If they knew they would have to stay all night, they might think twice.)
3. Do not get a girl pregnant. (Overall, that is just great advice at that age.)

I had no idea then that those three rules would have such an impact on those four boys or that they would take pride in following them. All I'd wanted was for them to think twice.

Years later, I saw that boy who'd had a troubled home life. He had become a man and he told me about the positive impact

I'd had on his life and how he had followed all of those rules, all the time, until he met a woman he loved. Then he broke rule #3 and had a baby.

Without even knowing it, and just by being yourself, you are impacting people who will impact the world. This is why it is so important to know your *Hell Yeah!*—so that you are in alignment as you are inadvertently impacting the world.

The Problem with Not Serving the World

If you don't vote you don't get to criticize what the people in charge do. The same applies to changing the world. If you don't increase your awareness of opportunities to change the world and look at how you can impact and embrace the actions that come from your thinking, then you don't get to criticize the state of the world. You just get to stay quiet and turn a blind eye. Once you know you can be a catalyst for change, you have a responsibility to step into your leadership.

By practicing critical thinking you will become the leader the world needs. We have too many leaders who are shortsighted, self-focused, irresponsible—and they are *running* things. They are running companies and organizations; they are teaching and coaching; and they are running our countries.

We need you to bring your awareness to the forefront, so step up and make changes where you can.

The Solution

You are not insignificant. You are not just a cog in the status quo machine. You are not too small.

We often think that we can't make an impact, that we are not important enough. If I told my friends who have quotes in this book that they were a big impact on the trajectory of my business, most of them probably wouldn't believe me.

Muhammad Ali had a massive reach. My friends don't have that kind of platform, but the domino effect they've had on me is massive. They have affected me, I am affecting you, and you are affecting other people. When we are done, we may not have Ali's fame, but we will have a lot of his reach.

For some reason, we are led to believe that we are less than we actually are, that our thoughts are not relevant or important, and so we think that means *we* are not relevant or important. Nothing could be further from the truth.

Our social system is set up for people to conform, but we need people to break away and lead the way in new and better directions. You are not the following type. You are the ground-breaking, leading type, and it's time you got excited about that role.

What are some ways you can learn to see things differently from a global perspective? You can read books or watch documentaries or travel. Those all provide different perspectives, but nothing is quite like travel. Traveling is such an important component to learning about and understanding the need to think critically. You cannot see poor people or their ways of doing things without thinking *something*. You don't always have to go far to gain the important effects of travel. If you live in the city, travel to the less fortunate areas of town. Talk with the people who live there. Get their views on life. If you can travel to Third World countries, then *do it*.

Travel is better than any self-help course, ever. The fastest way to improve who you are and get perspective is by looking at other people and how they live; talking to them and serving them—trying to understand them. Get outside of your usual, limited world. When you do, open your mind to consider that other perspectives are valid and important.

You cannot see someone else's world through your own eyes and be helpful. You must see *their* world through *their* eyes if you want to make the world better for *them*.

In Chapter 5 we discussed taking a look at what your customers need from their experience. Do the same for everyone you come in contact with. Leave your ego at the door, because this is not about you.

Let other people teach you things. Listen. Ask for their stories. Write them down so you can look back on them when you are wondering why you are doing what you're doing.

The world needs you. If you lead with your heart, check in with your head to make sure you are thinking. If you lead with your head, check in with your heart to make sure you are following your *Hell Yeah!* and helping, not hurting.

Domino Thinking

This Domino Thinking topic is in line with this chapter. When you are thinking about the scenario below, keep your business in mind. Consider how you impose your will. When do you think that your way is the best way? When people speak, do you really listen? Or just wait for your turn to talk? What is the outcome of all of those things?

A few years ago, I wanted to make a difference, so I looked into volunteer vacations. I have training to teach English as a second language and thought it might be nice to do some work in an orphanage. I was super excited to discover that I could go to a place where I could do that and also spend time at a lion reserve. The entire vacation was expensive, to the tune of $5,000 plus travel, but I thought it would be worth it.

I talked to a friend of mine from the country I was going to go to and he said the price was outrageous, as I could stay there like a queen for about $500 to $1000. That got me thinking about it all differently. Where was the money going? After doing some research, I saw articles about the increase in the number of orphanages popping up, and how daycares were being relabeled as orphanages to access Western dollars.

I realized then that I wanted to do that trip for me, not for them. I wanted to feel like a good person, but I wasn't going to leave good in my wake if I went on that trip. Volunteers like me were displacing local teachers; children were showing attachment disorders because of the transient nature of volunteers. How would contributing to that broken system be helping?

Spending that time thinking more deeply about what I was considering doing forced me to pull back the curtain and look at—I mean really look at—the difference between good intentions and good results.

Think about this: How does what you think about this situation apply in some way to your business? Come up with two ideas of how you are not actually helping when you think you might be.

Chapter 9
DUMP THE NAY-SAY

"Listen to other people with open ears and an open mouth, ready to call them an idiot if things go that way."
~ **Lea Silver**—my hope for the future

know this seems like an odd quote after all this empowering conversation, but I like it. I like it because sometimes we have to call people out on their "stuff" when we cannot sit passively and politely because we don't want to offend. If we don't speak up, we can hurt ourselves and our growth. Taking a position is important. Be firm. Know who you are.

Now that we have looked at different components of your business, we are going to go off in a different direction and look at a couple of other things. We do not live in a plastic bubble with our businesses and our lives. External forces impact us, but we need to keep facing forward. This chapter and the next one deal with the issues of other people's negative reactions and where you are going to go from here.

Whenever my son came home upset or bullied, I would tell him, "Don't let other people decide who you are." I wanted to be practical. I wanted to give the boy tools. Now I say the same thing to you: "Do not let other people decide who you are." Pause and think about that. Write it down.

Do not let other people decide who you are.

We are never going to get away from the criticism of others or the gremlins in our heads. The trick is to acknowledge them when they come up and try to look ahead to where the speed bumps are so you can develop a plan to deal with them.

Define the Negatives

I like to think about the negatives showing us how to formulate a plan. When we look at the negative it gives us more clarity about the positive.

If Jill is pitching a new idea and she knows that a certain member of her team is the most likely to have a problem with it, then knowing that going in will help Jill with her presentation. She can allow for the negativity and not get distracted by it. Maybe the negativity isn't about Jill's idea, but about that staff member feeling out of the loop. Maybe Jill can figure out a way to bring them into the loop first, even before the presentation.

When we realize that other people's negativity is about them it makes it easier to let it fall away. It's like the old saying: Other people's opinion of you is none of your business. However, that doesn't mean their nay-saying is easy to hear.

Yes, if you are a Buddhist monk and in such a state of enlightenment that you can be personally unaffected by the actions and words of another, then you can embrace that other people's opinions are none of your business and not feel the sting. If you are anything like me, it still hurts and makes an impact.

So try this the next time someone says something negative to you: Take a deep breath and say to yourself, "It's sad that they're having such a bad day." When we can move from insulted to compassionate, we shift the impact from negative to positive. We empathize with the other person. Sometimes I don't care if the other person is having a bad day. It's possible they are just an ass. The point of this exercise isn't to make them different, it is to make *you* different.

Start with your idea and look at all the reasons it might be a bad idea. Look at the rejections as well as the objections your own brain offers up. Look at those negatives and see if they are valid. Really look at them. Start with one and think about it and then reject or accept it. Move to another and reject or accept it. Go through all the possibilities. If, at the end of the process, you decide your course of action is a good one after all, then go for it.

If we take this approach when we are faced with adversity, two things happen. First, we are likely to feel confident about the direction we are taking and so we'll get less hung up on other people's opinions. Our brains will process those opinions and think, "Yep, I've heard that argument before and I worked through that solution." Second, if we bump up against an idea we haven't thought about yet, we are not exhausted from battling all the other nay-says and we are able to be open to hearing it.

It boils down to this: You get to decide who you are.

You

Let's face it, your thoughts are not always going to be good, and they are not always going to be popular. That doesn't mean you should stop thinking or stop talking about what you think.

Consider negative comments as a way to refine your thoughts, expand your thoughts, or dump your thoughts if they really do suck. Allow negative comments to be springboards to other, more brilliant, thoughts.

I remember one time I had a dream and when I woke up the next morning, I was so excited and the dream was still so fresh. I had a conversation with my friend that went something like this:

Me: Oh, man I just had the best dream ever. It would make a great movie

Friend: Tell me

Me: Okay. I was assigned the job of watching out for a dog who was in witness protection and was going to testify against the Mob.

Friend: (Looked at me like I had lost my mind.)

Me: Oh, that sounds insanely bad.

After saying the dream out loud, I realized how ludicrous it sounded, but I appreciated my friend's silent reproach. In my dream it *was* a great idea. In my head it *was* a great idea. In reality? Not so much.

On the other hand, there are times when you have a genuinely brilliant idea and someone close to you doesn't like it. At those times, you have to say thank you and remember that it's not about you and move forward.

You always get to decide who you are.

It can be hard to adapt to change. It is especially hard for people to accept change that either moves them in a direction they don't want to go or moves you in a direction they don't want you to go.

Change makes us vulnerable. But, man, oh man, there's fun in the journey. It is *not* fun to stay in the same place when your wings are wanting to take you farther.

More damaging than the opinions of others are the opinions in your own head. There is no magic formula to handle this. There are tools that you can use to try to help. You can make a list every day of your accomplishments (yes, putting the laundry away is an accomplishment). You can do a vision board of all the tough choices you've made and survived, or a vision board to remind you of where you want to go and what you want that journey to look like. You can name your little gremlin and have conversations with it, enlisting the help of other, more positive, voices in your head to talk your gremlin down. Find a way to live with your gremlins, as they are lifelong tenants inside your head.

The more negative talk you get from others and from yourself, the better your idea may be. Consider it a good sign and go forth with what makes your skin tingle.

Customers

Your customers are not all going to love you. They are going to say bad things sometimes to your face, sometimes to your staff, and sometimes all over Facebook for all the world to see.

You get to decide who you are.

The irony is that I am going through a really challenging situation with a client right now in the painting business. We did work for him. He agreed to the work. We gave him a discount and did some work for free to make up for something that didn't go according to plan.

Sadly, that wasn't enough for him and he is pulling random numbers from the air that he is wanting for a discount. I am faced with a situation of agreeing to his unreasonable requests or putting a lien on his house. At some point, it becomes about principles. I felt that if I accepted his ludicrous suggestion, it would tell him that the terrible things he is saying about my company and me were correct. I was not prepared to do that.

Being fair is one of my company's core beliefs, so it was extremely hard for me to have someone question that, and I spent a lot of time contemplating that belief.

I knew that customer was going to say terrible things about my company. But he'd have said horrible things anyway. I could not control that. When at the crossroads of a decision, I had to decide so that I wouldn't be the one telling myself terrible

things, since the voices in my head would be far more damaging than anything he could say.

Identify where the nay-say is coming from. Look at it, examine it, and hold it up against your *Hell Yeah!*. Breathe. Walk away from the problem. Breathe some more. Think some more. Make a decision that *you* can live with.

While you want to make your customer happy, it must be a win-win situation. If it is not, then either keep trying to make it a win-win or walk away.

Have you ever heard that there are only two outcomes, win-win and lose-lose? Win-lose is not an option, because if I am losing you cannot be winning and if you are losing I cannot be winning. Sometimes lose-lose is a choice you make.

If you are faced with an unreasonable client and you are trying to understand their perspective, ask yourself if you would do whatever it was they had done. If your answer is yes, then you have more work to do. If your answer is no, then take the necessary steps to protect yourself.

Staff

Hiring staff is a tricky thing. One disgruntled staff member can ruin the whole show. Nip that in the bud and fire their ass. When someone shows you who they are, believe them.

No staff member is so valuable that they have the right to sabotage your *Hell Yeah!* If they are, then you have bigger problems than them.

As you grow personally and professionally, you will tweak your *Hell Yeah!* and the people who work with you may not

embrace your changes. That is okay. Wish them well and send them packing.

There is no place in your business or on your team for someone who doesn't believe in where you are going and doesn't want to go there with you. You don't get to force them, because you don't get to decide who *they* are.

It is just as dangerous to have staff who agree with everything you say as to have disgruntled staff. In some situations, they may be the same thing. You can't grow in an environment where there is absolute compliance. There needs to be questioning. There needs to be honest conversation.

Keep in mind that there is a difference between a staff member who sabotages you and one who is saying things that make sense. Your first step is to listen and your second is to think.

It is important to create an environment in which your staff feel comfortable saying they don't agree, but also know they need to be a part of the solution or change. It is not enough to just point out a shortcoming—that is simply complaining. One must be part of the solution.

You get to decide who you are.

Community

Everyone in your community believes their cause or need is the most pressing and most important. You get to decide which of their causes are the most important to you and your *Hell Yeah!*

There will be people who are angry that you are not supporting them. Remember that you cannot please everyone. When you have a clear vision of your *Hell Yeah!*, then making

these kinds of choices is easier. When you are rejecting a cause it is sometimes easier for the asking party to accept that they don't fall into your mandate and you are not rejecting *them*.

Sometimes it is a good idea to find out what charities your colleagues support, because then maybe you can send good causes their way. Think about how a conversation with an asking charity is different when you say, "It is not my mandate to support little league, but I know of a company who does and is looking for a team to support." All of a sudden, you have given that charity a gift of a hot lead. That person who asked will hold you in higher regard because you helped when you didn't really need to.

You get to decide who you are.

The World

The world impacts us in ways we can't even fathom sometimes. It's easier to deal with if we have a filter in place.

You are ambushed by media trying to tell you what to buy, who to look like, how to be different from who you are. Music has meaning, yet we listen to it without acknowledging that, in doing so, we are perpetuating that music. For example, let's look at the song "Blurred Lines," by Robin Thicke. It's a catchy tune. It was banned by many universities for being misogynistic and promoting rape, because of its lyrics, such as "you know you want it" and "no doesn't always mean no." However, there is a very reasonable counterargument to be made that redefines all the lyrics in a context that means something different.

The question becomes, do you support the song? What happens if you do? Does everyone see the song as either inciting rape or empowering women? Or do people not listen to the words at all? What does your disapproval or endorsement of the song imply?

This song creates a great platform for conversation about how the world can be impacted by a seamlessly harmless thing like a song. Start talking about it.

We are impacted by politics and told by our peers who we should vote for and told by governments where it is safe to travel so we don't get caught in a terrorist attack. With all of that and more comes the world out there telling us what to do, think, and feel. Like Lea stated at the beginning of this chapter—you might have to tell someone they are an idiot and then proceed to making your own choice.

Don't let those voices get into your head and mess with your thinking. Look at situations and other people's opinions objectively. Even if they seem like they are directed at you or have implications for you, only *you* can decide if that is true.

You get to decide who you are.

The Solution

Stay in your own lane. I'm not talking about conforming, but about keeping your eyes off of what other people are doing. Let them do their own thing and focus instead on doing yours. This lesson of taking your own path and staying in your own lane becomes really clear if you walk a labyrinth. If you have never done one, I recommend you find one and walk it.

A friend of mine, Jivi, is brilliant about mindfulness. I went to one of her workshops and at the end she had us walk a chakra labyrinth. There were nine of us walking.

The lanes of a labyrinth are usually quite narrow. There is a single path that starts at the entrance on the outer edge and winds and twists into a center circle, where you stand and meditate, and then return along the circling, winding path back to the entrance, which is now your exit.

If you don't pay attention, you may wander out of your lane, end up headed in another direction, and even have the feeling you are a bit lost.

While you are walking, you are aware of other people on the labyrinth, but you cannot focus too much on them or you will lose your focus on where you are going. Sometimes you pass someone going the other direction in the lane next to you and you have to stay focused on your lane as you squeeze past each other. Sometimes you have to step out of the way to let someone walk past you on your own lane.

The other people are there, but at the same time they are not important to your journey. This thinking stuff, your business stuff, functions in the same way. Pick your lane. Pay little attention to what other people are doing when it comes to deciding who you are and where you're headed. Know where you are going or, at the very least, where you want to end up.

The interesting thing is that when you are standing at the entrance of a labyrinth, looking at the center, you cannot visually trace the path you will take. You can try, but it's confusing and the lanes backtrack. You don't need to know the path. You just need to trust that the path will get you where you need to go. Then, with that trust, you start walking.

The other people sharing the labyrinth are on their own paths with their own agendas. They may bump up against you, politely make arrangements together to solve the problem to avoid a crash, and then you both carry on.

Walking a labyrinth is a metaphor for your business and your life. You get to appreciate the other people doing their things while you continue to build and work on your own *Hell Yeah!*.

You get to decide who you are.

Domino Thinking

Think about the situation below and see how you may be using the same thinking in your life. See if there are other ways to look at things.

In Cambodia, there is a lot of poverty (poverty is not unique to Cambodia, but I had to pick a place for this exercise and I have been there and I loved it). Due to the degree of poverty, families must do what they can to survive. This often means having children selling items or asking for money to buy milk (which is a scam, by the way).

Time and time again, if there is an adult selling bracelets at a location and a child nearby selling the same thing, most tourists will buy from the child, thinking they are doing them more of a favor.

The smarter thing to do is to buy from the adult, but our instinct is to help the poor child. Here's why it is a bad idea. When that child continues to make money, the family cannot afford to let them stop to go to school. This maintains the poverty cycle and the lack of education that keeps Cambodians poor. When the adults are the ones making the money, the kids have no financial value on the street, and education holds more long-term value.

Another common mistake tourists make is to take pictures of children. Sometimes the parents will ask for money for this, thus creating an economy around the child again. Even if there is no one to ask for payment, that child is still being objectified. We wouldn't go up to an adult and shove a camera in their face, and yet we think that's okay to do to children.

Why do we do these things?

What is the long-term effect of these choices?

How can we better contribute?

You may never go to Cambodia or any other Third World country (although I highly recommend it), but you can still ask yourself where you might be doing these same sorts of things in your life. Where do you see other people do these sorts of things? What can you do about it?

Think about this: How does what you think about this situation apply in some way to your business? Come up with two ideas of ways you overlook your impact.

Chapter 10
FLY, BABY, FLY

"No one is a nobody to everybody. So be someone. Be you."
— **Line Brunet**— radio host

You were not born to sit on the sidelines. If you think you were, you are mistaken. You were born to shine and to impact the world in marvelous ways.

My Wish for You

I know you want to make a difference, and you will. You do. The way to do that will show up in unique ways. Don't misunderstand me—I know that a version of everything has been done before—but what *hasn't* been done is *your* way of doing things.

We often under-emphasize our own flair. Have you ever heard someone say something and think nothing of it and then later hear someone else say it in a slightly different way that makes you think to yourself, "Wow! That makes so much sense."

We don't all hear the same way or process the same things or learn in the same manner. You are going to be uniquely suited to *someone*. If you are unique to someone, then you can be unique to more people.

You are capable of doing all the wonderful things swimming around in your head and your soul. What I wish for you is to go after it *all*. See your journey as being on that labyrinth and know that the path will take you where you want to go. Trust yourself. Trust that little voice in your head telling you whether something is a good idea or *isn't* a good idea. Know what your *Hell Yeah!* is and don't stop following it with all the passion it deserves.

What's Next?

The ideas in the book and the practice of using Domino Thinking can become a part of your personal life and your business life.

Use what you have read here as a way to open conversations with your staff, your family, your mentors, your community, the world. Ask people what they think. Teach your children and your nieces and nephews to think about what *they* think about. Spread the need to *Think Opposite* to your community.

Challenge yourself to make critical thinking part of your life. Practice.

Know that when you change, others around you can't help but change. Simply by *being* different, the people around you will be different. Gandhi didn't set out to have the impact he did on the world. He just went along being who he was and stayed aligned with his belief system. The world saw that, and the world changed.

Stay in Touch: I Want to Know

I am a little bit sad to be leaving you now, as you go forward to make big differences in your life and to those in your life. I love a good adventure and for sure, life is an adventure. I wonder what yours will be? It's waiting for you. You really can make magic happen.

I invite you to share your *Hell Yeah!* with me, along with your comments, your questions, and your good, bad, beautiful, and ugly parts. Because you made it this far in the book, I would totally dig working with you to uncover those things further.

You can send me your comments and criticisms (because that way I will grow too) on www.dominothinking.com /lets-talk.

From time to time, you will find freebies on my website, www.dominothinking.com, just to keep you thinking and to keep you pushing the limits of what you think you know.

Domino Thinking

This is your last Domino Thinking section. I hope you have enjoyed them and they have given you interesting things to think and talk about. You can come up with your own and share them with me and other people. Keep the thinking and questioning alive.

How often have you, in your business or personal life, accepted a word into your vocabulary and made it a part of your conversations without really knowing what that word means to you?

Obviously, some words have more power than others. But some of the words we use have tremendous power and connotation. How aware you of those words that you use?

Let's look at the word *feminism*. We all use the word. We all have feelings when we hear the word. What does it actually mean, and beyond that, what does it mean to you?

At best, I had a dubious relationship with the word *feminism*. I was a woman in the trades, I was a single mom, and my gut reaction to the term *feminism* was that it was said as an insult. It was linked to man-hating lesbians and, as it so happened, I was neither. I felt I had to apologize and explain to people that I wasn't a feminist. I did all of that with very little consciousness.

Then one day, my ex-boyfriend was telling me a story about a woman who had been told by a man that she "owed" him for her job, which he had gotten for her, and he expected sex. The man was confronted about that comment and apologized. I asked my ex how the woman felt about that outcome. He sneered at me a bit and said in a condescending tone, "Why would she care, and when did you become such a feminist?" I promptly responded with indignation "I am *not* a feminist."

I was really bothered by that whole situation for the following reasons:

1. Someone had, yet again, used the word *feminism* to insult me.
2. I wondered why wanting to know how she felt about the sexual assault made me anything other than simply concerned.
3. I wondered why I had such a strong reaction to the word.
4. It occurred to me that maybe it was time I had a better understanding of a word that had such an impact on me and others.

Querying *feminism* created a really interesting journey for me. I started having conversations with people about what they thought about that word. I gave speeches on why it seemed to be considered a "four-letter word."

The *Merriam-Webster Learner's Dictionary* defines feminism as: "the belief that men and women should have equal rights and opportunities" and "the theory of the political, economic and social equality of the sexes" (learnersdictionary.com/definition/feminism).

Wow. Not confusing. Yet, true to form, society has created all of this "stuff" around this term. Nowhere does the definition say that only women can be feminists. Or that men should be oppressed so that women can be equal. Or… or… or…

Tell me, what is your relationship with the word *feminism*?

Do you know how other people in your life feel about feminism?

Start asking them. Start some conversations about this term and its complex effect on our society.

And once you have done that, ask yourself what other terms—ones you maybe don't really know the definition of, or your relationship to—you have accepted into your life without examining? What industry terms are you using that you haven't given much thought to? Maybe "best practices"? What makes them the best practices? Or "bottom line"? Have you explored what that means to you?

Stop accepting such words into your life without examining them. Become mindful of the concepts you don't really understand and yet are employing in your language.

Think about this: How does what you think about this apply in some way to your business? Come up with two terms you use without really understanding them.

––––––––

I leave you with this thought:
Your business can be more than just a way to make money.
It can be used as a tool to change the world.

ACKNOWLEDGEMENTS

Thanks, to Lisa Fettinger Smith for her encouraging words when I needed them most. To my Michigan peeps—I love you much and have learned so much about the power of friendship! To Angela Lauria at The Author Incubator, for believing in my idea for this book. To Grace Kerina for being my supportive editor. Of course to the people listed below for inspiring me.

As you know, I have used quotes from people in my life who have made an impact. In case you're interested in knowing more about that, I'll share here a bit about how those people have affected me:

Tone Donaghey is my son. He quite possibly saved my life. I didn't always make good choices and was heading down a rather unsavoury path before I became pregnant. I love being his mom. He is the most kind and gentle man I know. He has all the best parts I am missing.

Eric Gilmer is my oldest and dearest friend. I met him while taking criminology classes. Eric always has had an undying opinion that I am brilliant, even when evidence has suggested otherwise. He is the truly gifted writer of our duo and I hope with all of my heart that he one day graces the world with his words. I will keep pushing him.

Jivi Saran is my storyteller. I could sit and listen to her for hours. Oh, wait, I do! Jivi is the most mindful person I know. She has taught me the benefits of serenity—even when we are swearing. I am so looking forward to going to India with her in 2017 and getting this body, soul, and brain of mine enlightened. (www.thecorporatementalist.ca)

Marc Stoiber is a spectacular speaker and a marketing genius. He believed in me enough to help me create my Ultimate Speech. He is my exposure to ultimate collaboration and his enthusiasm is contagious. (www.marcstoiber.com)

Anel Bester was my coach. During my first meeting with her, she called me out on my business and my purpose—and there were still 50 minutes left in that hour-long session. She kicks ass and tells it like it is, with an undying enthusiasm for my gifts. Her pursuit of greatness is admirable. (www. anelbester.com)

Tanya O'Rourke has been my roommate since 1999. She moved in for a month and became family. She has been here for me through poorly chosen boyfriends, deaths, and celebrations. She will always be my friend. She has an incredibly vulnerable way of looking at herself, seeing what needs changing, and then slowly heading in the direction of who she wants to be. I am so proud of her.

Audrea Hooper I met at a speakers' retreat, and I was so moved by her passion for the company she works for and by her speech about the importance of feeling like she matters to them. Her speech got me thinking in all different directions, which I love. I knew I needed a quote from her for this book. She is a living example of why thinking matters. Audrea is the Head of Fungineering (www.zappos.com).

Gina Best became a friend quickly. After meeting her, I fell in love just a little bit. She is fierce and powerful and has a vulnerability that requires immense courage. She took me into her circle of friends and I am better for the experience. (www.gina.best)

Todd Sinclair is someone I had to go all the way to Cambodia to meet. He was a tour leader with G Adventures for a group of us going through Cambodia. His compassion for the people and his dedication to our experience was life altering for me. We spent one fabulously, horribly drunk night on Pub Street in Siem Reap on St Patrick's Day and have stayed in touch ever since. He is my inspiration for living life to its fullest and my call for more kindness. He makes me want to be a better person. (www.gadventures.com)

Lea Silver was my assistant for six months. She is young, an entrepreneur, and my hope for the next generation. When I see her brilliance, her focus, and her certainty about who she is and what she wants, I am humbled by how long it took me to get to that vicinity. At 23, she is already there. If anyone ever says the next generation is entitled or lazy, etc., Lea is a shining example of how utterly untrue those statements are. (www.roarrepresentation.com)

Line Brunet It was Line who, after hearing me speak for the first time, told me she almost cried at how great she thought I was, and then promptly told me I needed to make a business out of all this thinking stuff. (www.linebrunet.com)

All of these people have played a part in shaping me and in shaping this book. They are extraordinarily ordinary people who somehow I got lucky enough to be on the same speck of dirt with. With every fibre of my being and every fragment of my soul, I thank them.

ABOUT THE AUTHOR

Alison Donaghey has always been an opposite thinker. She used to think that made her more of an annoyance than an asset. In the process of starting her house-painting company, Sonshine Girls Painting, she realized that thinking opposite is an asset and used it more and more. That put her on a fast track to becoming one of the best-known companies in the area. In a few years, she went from a single mom on welfare to making over six figures.

Alison's commitment to thinking opposite prompted her to start another business, Domino Thinking, which challenges people to think about what they think about. As an author, speaker, and thought strategist, she encourages people to question the status quo and apply their own opposite thinking to improve not only *their* world but *the* world.

Alison has been fortunate enough to create a life that allows her to travel—alone or with her son—and learn from other cultures. She's a big fan of trying everything once, be it skydiving, eating crickets, bungee jumping, white water rafting, or walking with lions. Not everything bears a second try, but it's hard to have regrets if everything is tried at least once.

Alison currently lives on Vancouver Island, on the west coast of British Columbia, in a house she designed and living a life she is constantly redesigning. Life is good.

Would You Like Me To Personally Help
You Get Clear In Your Business, For Free?

Dear Friend,

I'm looking for a "dream" client … one that I can bring massive in windfalls for.

If you're that client, then I will personally help you create a strategic plan For FREE!

You heard me … I am going to help you 100% for free. The first thing I am personally going to do for you is take a close look at your business and develop a strategic plan for you to take it to the next level.

There's no charge for this and it only takes 45-90 minutes for us to do together

How Will I Get You These Boldly Claimed Results?

What's the key to taking your business from where it is now, to where you want it to be?

Sales, marketing, quality of your product… they all factors in, but none of that matters if you don't have one thing…

A clear understanding of what you are doing and why you are doing it. That will solve almost every problem you will ever have.

So if you want to:

✓ Be more efficient

✓ Attract the clients who are best for your company (not every client is a profitable client)

✓ Reduce expensive staff turnover by meeting the needs of your staff

✓ Save money contributing to community in ways that don't support your business

✓ Make a bigger impact with your business so you can leave a legacy that lasts forever

✓ Create time for some work life balance so you won't have to miss your kid's baseball game or so you can be home in time for dinner with your family

Then I will personally help you get there!

Here's How It Will Work

First off, we get on the phone one on one and go over your business.

I take a look at what you got, what you're doing, and what you want to achieve going forward.

Once we have those raw materials, I'll help you come up with a strategic plan to get you to where you want to be.

There are two things that can happen:

1. **You love the plan** and decide to implement it on your own. In that case, I'll wish you the best of luck and I ask that you keep in touch with me and let me know how you're doing.
2. **You Love the plan and you ask to become my client so I can personally help you execute it for maximized results.**

In that case, we will kill it together! All of my clients get results… literally every single one. And you will be no different

It really is that simple and there is no catch—Zero, Zip, Nada, Zilch!

Why Would I Offer This?

There's actually two reasons:

The first is that I truly love helping people get clear on their businesses so they can take them to the next level.

Selfish or not, I just love seeing the results I can get for people.

The second reason is…

It's how I attract my dream clients. On the phone call I **might** decide that you meet the criteria (I'm super picky and I want to work with people I can help).

Here's how that works:

Assuming you're happy with the value I provided you over the phone, you will probably want to continue working with me long term.

In that case, I might invite you to become a client.

My "fees" start at $2,500. It includes a 5 phase plan to:

- Get you clear on why you are doing what you are doing
- How to attract loyal customers and understand you points of contact with you clients
- Get your staff on board and understand their why
- Contribute to your community in a way that will best position your company and your reason for being in business

We can add to this

- A VIP day where I work with you or your staff to get "inside" your company prior to the 5 phase plan
- Speaking workshops to engage your staff in activities to start applying these principles

OR

- Hire me to speak at your next conference with fees starting at $1500

And when you consider the results, this will get you to:

- ✓ Be more efficient
- ✓ Attract the clients who are best for your company (not every client is a profitable client after all)
- ✓ Reduce expensive staff turnover by meeting the needs of your staff

✓ Save money contributing to community in ways that don't support your business

✓ Make a bigger impact with your business so you can leave a legacy that lasts forever

✓ Create time for some work life balance so you won't have to miss your kid's baseball game or so you can be home in time for dinner with your family

Because of the results, it literally pays for itself in the first day!

And here's my giant promise to you…

This Is NOT For Everybody… Here's Who I Can Help:

Again, like I said, I am only looking for my dream client. So I'm going to be extra picky.

You must:

1. **Already have 10+ employees** (I'm not looking to work with some startup… and NO solopreneurs)
2. **You must already be bringing in six figures a year**
3. You must be willing to accept change (It's amazing how hard that is for some people)
4. **You must follow directions.** Meaning you must be willing to put in the work and actually execute the plans and strategies we come up with. (Don't worry, I wont ask you to jump off a cliff or anything like that)

5. You must have a good solid product. **I just can't afford to stand behind some substandard product or service.** My goal isn't just to help you, but bring massive value to your customers and the market place.
6. **You have to actually care about your employees.** I'm NOT here to help you make money at their expense. I only work in win-win environments.
7. And you must have a super cool personality. **(We're going to be spending some time together, so let's have some fun.**

That's it! Those are all of my requirements!
Now that we got that out of the way...

Here's What I Want You To Do Next

If you meet my obnoxiously picky criteria above and you would like me to personally get you those results I promised, then I would be more than happy to set aside time for you.

Here's how the process works:

Go to the website below

www.BookAlison.Today

You will be asked to fill out a application... don't worry it will take you less than 60 seconds and it's just basic questions that will help me get a feel for your business.

I also ask for a deposit of $500

Don't worry... I could care less about your money.

I'm just using it as a filter so only serious people will schedule a time to talk.

The second we get off the phone I'll give you every dime back. (Unless I take you on as a client-in that case I will subtract it from your total balance)

What Will Happen After That?

Once you have made the initial "qualifying" deposit (which you will get back immediately following the call)

You will be taken to a page where you will be able to schedule a time that works for the both of us.

I will review you application and we will get on the phone for 45-90 minutes.

In that time we are going to take a look at where your business is and where you want it to be. We will take an in depth look at every aspect of your business and determine what needs to happen in order to get it to the next level.

If you see the value in becoming one of my clients, great! We can talk about it.

However, *if you don't want to become a client, that's OK too!*

But here's the thing...

WARNING: TIME IS A FACTOR

Getting on these calls is a very time consuming process, and even if I could take them all day, **I only have the time to work with a few of my dream clients.**

You see, when I work with a client I like to pour my heart and soul into it.

That means I can only take on a handful of clients… and *they have to be the perfect fit.*

So you need to hurry!

If you want to have the opportunity to get on the phone with me… for FREE

Then you need to go to **www.BookAlison.Today** right now.

You should realize that there is high demand for one-on-one attention from me and what I'm offering right now is unprecedented.

So with that said, know that your opportunity will be completely wasted if you don't get out your phone or computer right now and go to

>>> www.BookAlison.Today <<<

A free eBook edition is available with the purchase of this book.

To claim your free eBook edition:

1. Download the Shelfie app.
2. Write your name in upper case in the box.
3. Use the Shelfie app to submit a photo.
4. Download your eBook to any device.

Shelfie

A free eBook edition is available
with the purchase of this print book.

CLEARLY PRINT YOUR NAME ABOVE IN UPPER CASE

Instructions to claim your free eBook edition:
1. Download the Shelfie app for Android or iOS
2. Write your name in **UPPER CASE** above
3. Use the Shelfie app to submit a photo
4. Download your eBook to any device

Print & Digital Together Forever.

Snap a photo

Free eBook

Read anywhere

www.TheMorganJamesSpeakersGroup.com

We connect Morgan James published authors with live and online events and audiences whom will benefit from their expertise.

Morgan James
Speakers Group

Morgan James makes all of our titles available
through the Library for All Charity Organizations.

www.LibraryForAll.org